A House for Two Pounds

K. IGGULDEN

(NÉE KATHLEEN MORAN)

A House for Two Pounds

MICHAEL JOSEPH
an imprint of
PENGUIN BOOKS

MICHAEL JOSEPH

UK | USA | Canada | Ireland | Australia
India | New Zealand | South Africa

Michael Joseph is part of the Penguin Random House group of companies
whose addresses can be found at global.penguinrandomhouse.com.

Penguin
Random House
UK

First published 2019
001

Copyright © K. Iggulden, 2019

The moral right of the author has been asserted

Set in 9.25/12.5 pt Sabon LT Std
Typeset by Jouve (UK), Milton Keynes
Printed and bound in Great Britain by Clays Ltd, Elcograf S.p.A.

A CIP catalogue record for this book is available from the British Library

HARDBACK ISBN: 978–0–241–41782–9

www.greenpenguin.co.uk

To the people and places of my childhood

Introduction

A love of Ireland and the Irish is what shines through this little book. It looks back to families and villages around Cork in what might have been a vanished age, but in her hands is just around the corner, across the fields. My mother's childhood in the 1930s involved two or three generations – her parents, her brother and sisters, all those around them. The children and grandchildren of those people are still with us – indeed, I am one. I think that love is what she wanted me to understand. She saw her people as intensely polite, decent and innocent, with humour and music always ready. She saw them as poets, and poetry as the highest art. She admired them, no, she *adored* them. How many of us can say that of the people we knew in our youth?

On reading these stories, I am left with a quiet reverence for those who went before – for their laughter and songs, for their faith and dislike of cold authority, their quiet resilience. Yes, there is tragedy and loss, but what remains, as I close the book, is peace and a memory of kindness. These were good people – and surprisingly funny ones. Their stories are worth telling because all lives are, because the past is a place our parents and grandparents met, not some strange valley beyond our understanding. I stood by the house my grandfather built just last summer, looking out over the fields. The door was sticking and the day was cold, but it's all just a step away.

The creation of these chapters is a story in itself. Though she was born Kathleen Moran, I knew my mother as Kathy Iggulden, teacher of English and history in north London, lover of poetry and song, and as fierce an advocate for her children as it is possible to be. Identity is a strange and shifting thing. She wrote these interlocking pieces for years, changing some things, adding others or taking them out, deciding what could at last be revealed and what kept secret. She struggled for a long time with revealing her past in Ireland, though she came to terms with it in the end and was at ease. It is a happy childhood for the most part. Her love and trust in people can be felt on every page – which is how I remember her.

When you are growing up, almost anything can become normal. For me, that was coming home from school to find some stranger in my house who needed a room for a few days or a few months. My mother would get talking to someone on a train or in a shop and they'd tell her all their troubles. They seemed to sense her compassion and we never had a year without someone in the spare room, sorting their life out. Those were the informal ones, the lost chickens my mother would find. More formally, a succession of young women came to stay with us to have a baby they could not keep, then went home, to Ireland, Malta, Sweden or Japan, as soon as the child had been born and adopted. My father used to say the neighbours looked on him in astonishment at the parade of pregnant ladies going in and out of ours.

I understand a little better now that my mother felt it was not enough just to have a warm house, a loving husband and children. She felt she had to do something for those who had not been given as much, in the most practical way possible. She was always involved in some good work and sent money all around the world. Nor was that enough. Unusually, she tried to live her help. If it was counselling a friend whose marriage was in trouble, or hiding a woman whose violent husband was searching for her, that was what she did. If there was ever a lack of certainty in her, I did not see it. Right was right. My father put up with a great deal of strangeness, but he was so amazed at his luck in finding her that he hardly ever complained.

On one occasion, when she answered the phone to a heavy breather, she demanded to know his reasons for wasting her time in such a way. After a torrent of questions, the man at the other end began rather sheepishly to answer. She kept him on the phone for an hour after that until he had assured her he would mend his ways and turn his life around.

She trusted people and expected the best of them. I used to think that was perfectly normal, but the wonderful thing was how often they stepped up and tried to meet her expectations. She was, for example, the worst parker of cars it has ever been my privilege to witness. She would abandon them like a ship offshore – so far from the kerb that the entire road would come to a halt in astonishment. Time and time again, her preferred method was to call a passing young man, hand him the keys and ask him to park it for her. I used to plead with her not to do it, saying that someone would surely steal the car. Yet no one ever did. Pleased and proud to be asked, they parked it neatly to a man and went on.

My mother loved men. She understood instinctively that they were the weaker sex, but that it was vital never to let them know you knew. 'Do you realise? Women are in *charge!*' she told her sister, in the way of sharing an astonishing secret. I asked her once why she, a highly intelligent woman, had to ask Dad to wire a plug. She said it made him happy to do things like that for her – and why would she take that away from him?

She was also the worst cook I have ever known, though the reason for that is in this book and will become clear. When I was a young boy, I thought fudge was something that could break like glass and be sucked. Lasagne was a sort of thick biscuit and the kitchen itself was a dangerous place, where things exploded and ricocheted off the ceiling. In the end, my father took over the cooking completely. He said he had the highest charcoal content in his blood of any man in England and just could not take it any more.

It was a happy childhood, because my English father and Irish mother adored each other and made our home a place of laughter. I know I delighted in making my mother laugh, more than just about anything.

She passed on a love of words: of poetry and history. She loved the English verses of Tennyson, and she loved the Irish verses of Yeats – just about equally, as far as I could tell. Neither was allowed to overshadow the other and both could make her gasp and shake her head at the perfection of a line. She kept half a dozen chickens in a suburban garage in Eastcote, Middlesex, because she missed them from her childhood.

Her faith, too, was a thing of wonder. I sometimes thought it was odd that we had to sing whenever we passed a Catholic church: 'Praise to the Holiest in the height, And in the depth be praise.' I know *now* that it isn't something other people do and probably never was, but she enjoyed it and she liked to hear us sing. For my mother, faith and trust in God were much like breathing – a vital part of her. She always worried she had not done enough to pass it on to us. I remember arguing over some aspect of the Immaculate Conception when I was a great lout of a young man – and suddenly realising that I could *not* win, that if I scored a point against her faith, I would be undermining the very heart of her, the wellspring. I retired from the field, though the truth is, I was never in much danger of succeeding anyway.

I taught with her just once, in the same classroom, for the last term of my own training. I was pleased to have the chance. After all, I'd known a hundred strangers hail my mother, men and women who'd recognise her from some old school and come over in delight.

It brought her joy and satisfaction to pass on knowledge, so it was never a surprise to hear she'd started to tutor a foreign priest, or a neighbour's daughter. Of course, her sons bore the brunt of that desire to teach, for their *entire* lives. I appreciate it more now than I did in my teenage years! Romantic tales and poetry snatched from thin air and recited in reams. She made me understand that history was nothing more or less than the stories of those good people gone on before.

She told me of Napoleon throwing open his cloak to an army, revealing his medals, daring them to arrest him. She always had a soft spot for the little Corsican. Nothing we could say would change her mind.

To her last days, she never gave up chipping away at her sons, reminding them to shave, to polish our shoes, to watch our weight, to buy flowers for wives if we had them, to try not to be impatient. She understood our faults and worked always to improve them, but reminded us: ''Twixt the saddle and the ground, mercy sought and mercy found' – that we were to pray for salvation even in the final moments.

I wrote this for her, when I was around twenty-six or so.

To My Mother

I am not yet the man I want to be,
There's so much more to make, to want, to do,
But everything I'm proud of that's in me,
Is something that I saw at first in you.

4

I learned from you how not to fear the crowd,
To never be content to be a sheep,
To think before unthinkingly to bow,
To stand straight, take a breath and leap.

You read the words of men who lay in tombs,
And read them like they lived and watched you shine,
You spoke and light was in the rooms,
And I knew Arthur Hallam through the lines.

I learned to think of God on wooden pew,
And though my wand'rings sometimes make you sad,
I struggle meeting standards set by you
(In truth, I think old Jesus struggles too)
But I know right from wrong – and good from bad.

I work with word and wind and wood and song,
And though I've not seen Ireland now for years,
The shadow of its spirit's long,
And warms the ground as winter nears.

I cannot pay the first of what I owe,
You chose this life and my life came about,
My greatest thanks as through the world I go,
For I can meet the battle with a shout.

Ten months after Dad's death, she was taken into hospital and drifted into sleep in no pain and without fear. I combed her hair for her, the only time I ever thought to do it. Also, the last. At her funeral, I read the following words of Henry van Dyke as part of her eulogy:

A ship spreads white sails into the morning breeze. I stand and watch until she hangs as a speck between sea and sky – and someone says: 'There. She is gone.'

And at that moment, when someone at my side says, 'She is gone,' there are other eyes watching for her arrival – and glad voices are raised to shout: 'Here she comes. There she is!'

Hers was a good death – and a better life. When we came to look for her will, we found she had written these words on the outer envelope:

> God Bless you all. Dad and I are happy now, for evermore with God. Be good men. Strive to be compassionate, kind, helpful to others and dedicated to your family. Time is precious – use it well. We loved you and we want to meet again in Heaven, so keep the commandments. Remember the Grace of God is in courtesy – and God save Ireland.

(My father then added, 'And England', to which she replied, 'Yes, yes, yes, of course.')

C. Iggulden

PART ONE

I

As I Remember Brookedale

Ireland has a strange, poignant way of holding on to her children. Not time, nor oceans, nor a thinning of the blood through intermarriage can weaken the bonds that bind her to her versatile family. I grew up in a friendly corner of Munster, County Cork. Ballinona, within cycling distance of the sea, rolls through the green south to the small town of Midleton and shelters a people whose warmth, wit and camaraderie left an indelible impression on my youthful self. These are my people – I need no interpreter to know their values, and it seems to me they open their mouths in poetry.

In June 1932, my father cycled to a fair in Listowel with hope and relief in his heart. He had been up all night awaiting the birth of a new baby. He was a young, hard-working farmer, who had naturally hoped for a son to follow him on the land. He already had a small daughter whom he dearly loved, but a boy would have crowned all his hopes and desires.

Soon after midnight of the day before, a grey-faced, exhausted mid-wife had entered the kitchen, coming down from his wife's bedroom.

'Con,' she said, 'I'm sorry – the baby girl was stillborn and I fear your wife is sinking. We cannot stem the bleeding. Run now, please, for the village doctor and the priest.'

Instantly, he rushed away to fetch both men. The situation was particularly tragic for my father because his own mother had died in childbirth when he was just nine. His father – the local seannachie, or storyteller, in the days before television or even radios – had often gathered together a group of neighbours to exchange views and tales, with a little singing thrown in. On one such evening, when darkness had fallen and only the murmur of voices and the occasional laugh broke the silence, a knock was heard at the back door of the old thatched farmhouse. That door was always left unlocked and a middle-aged woman entered. As was customary at the time (and typical of Irish hospitality), the woman was seated and given tea and buttered bread. No one knew her and she volunteered no information about herself or her background.

After an hour's rest, she rose to leave and my grandfather escorted her to the door. As she opened it, she took a small brown envelope from her pocket and handed it to him. It contained a white powder, collected into one corner.

She said, 'Thank you for your hospitality. I can do this for you in return. Keep this envelope safely. If you do not, I tell you now in warning, three people will die in your family.'

Now my grandfather was not a superstitious man, but the woman's fierce earnestness alarmed him. He decided not to keep the powder in the house. Instead, he loosened a brick in an outhouse by the back door and stuck the envelope behind it.

A few months later, it was Easter. Like all good Catholics, my grandfather went to Confession and told the story to the priest of the woman's dark warning. The priest was furious and blamed him for taking any notice of her. Furthermore, the priest said he would not give him absolution for his sins until he brought the envelope to the church to be destroyed. Grandfather hurried away to get it, but found to his dismay that it had vanished without trace. A month later, his wife died in childbirth, along with the twins she carried.

Back in the kitchen, where my father remembered those unhappy events, his reverie was interrupted by the emergence of the doctor from above. Where there had been cries of pain before, there was only silence. My father feared the worst.

'Con!' the doctor called, in his booming voice. 'I have good news for you. Nora will live this time. Your wife is weak, but she will recover.'

'And the baby?'

As my father spoke, the piercing shriek of a newborn came from the bedroom. The doctor looked up in astonishment. After delivery, believing the child was dead and expecting the imminent demise of her mother, he and the midwife had rolled the baby in an old towel and placed her out of sight at the foot of the bed. That baby was me – and it seems that after a rest, I found my voice and yelled for attention. I continued to be a very noisy baby and was referred to as 'our June screecher' for the next year or so.

Whether it was the first certainty that I was dead or the near-miraculous recovery, my father always treated me as special. Although he tried to be fair and loving to all his children, and eventually to the precious son, Joe, I knew the depth of his love for me and, of course, exploited it shamelessly.

That was why he whistled as he cycled along the following morning, on the way to the fair at Listowel. He said later, that he smiled at the morn, for joy.

'Do you like this wine?' I asked my young Irish cousin in a fairly exclusive London restaurant. He wrinkled his nose doubtfully.

'I fear there isn't a song in a bucket of it,' he replied.

The phrase took me back to harvest threshing-days in Ballinona and the songs that lightened the evenings. One of Ballinona's beauty spots was a hilltop farm called Brookedale. There I grew up, with my two sisters and my brother, Joe. Our parents, who met at the Rose of Tralee Festival, came from Kerry and Limerick respectively. They bought Brookedale in 1937, and for the rest of their lives kept a nostalgic corner of their hearts for the soft-spoken people of the west. My father, Con Moran, belonged to the sixth generation of farmers in his family and it was his dearest wish that my brother should succeed him. Daddy played the fiddle and the flute and had such an extensive repertoire of songs that it was difficult to conclude any casual conversation with him without sudden melodious contributions – as words sparked off memories.

'I've a new friend at school,' I'd tell him, and he'd sing, 'May your friends be true when needed – may you never feel as we did . . .'

As I went out of the door, the songs would follow me down the avenue. As my name is Kathleen, I was greeted several times a day with 'Kathleen Mavourneen', or 'I'll Take You Home Again, Kathleen' or even 'Dear Old Donegal', which mentions 'kissing your sister Kate'. He was, without exception, the most cheerful man I have ever known. He rose with the first light and whistled as he laced his shoes. My mother, Nora Holly, of a much more introverted temperament, loved him all her life. Though she was quick-witted and perceptive, she was slower of speech and movement than my father. As he often waited for her before they went out, he referred to her affectionately as 'my lagging love'[1] – and hummed a few bars of that famous touching melody to entertain us.

My elder sister was and still is called Mauraid, though now she has the prefix 'Sister' to her name. Such an addition was regarded as a unique blessing by my mother and as an insurance by my father. In later years, he kept a copy of a simple poem, 'I'm the Daddy of a Nun', by his bedside until he died. The poet presented a picture of a man of the world sauntering up to Heaven's gates to have his failings scrutinised by St Peter. The man, the poet says, has nothing to fear. The gates will open wide for him if he just 'whispers to St Peter "I'm the Daddy of a Nun"'.

My younger sister and the prettiest of us all was Mary. She was the perfect daughter – loyal and faithful and, above all, there. She was there when they lost all their money and later – a skilled, experienced nurse, she was there with them both at the end, while the rest of us crossed oceans to be with them and only half made it.

Money was very scarce when we were young. My parents never gave us pocket money but we were encouraged to earn a little by doing some of the hundred and one jobs around the farm. There was a large field below the house in which tall, green and yellow 'weeds' flourished. Far from using weed-killer, which would have poisoned the soil, my father engaged the four of us to pull them up. He paid us a penny a hundred, which wasn't as miserable a pay as it sounds.

As each of us reached the age of about twelve, we were given a newborn calf to care for, to watch over and to sell when it was a yearling. Mine was a little red-brown bull with a wavy coat and huge liquid eyes

1 A reference to 'My Lagan Love' – an old Irish love-song.

fringed about with blue-black curly lashes that any girl might envy. The little calf was taken from his mother within hours of birth and I fed him from a bucket half full of her rich yellow milk. He learned to drink from this by sucking my fingers, which I plunged into the warm liquid. At twelve, I was a bit nervous that he might bite but I soon learned that the cavern of his mouth held no dangers. He had no teeth and cows never grow more than one set anyway. His long, rough tongue used to tickle my small hand and I thought he was trying to swallow it.

He was kept, with three or four others, in the calf house for six weeks and fed, mostly by me, three times a day. I suppose one of the most desolate sounds in the world is that of a cow-mother bellowing soulfully for her calf. Yet when the calves went out into the fields, after six or eight weeks, their mothers appeared to have forgotten them. I watched over the growth of my calf with fascinated affection, not because he was cash on the hoof – unimaginable amounts of it, as far as I was concerned – but because he knew me. I fancied he gambolled clumsily in youthful springs when I entered his field.

I made endless plans for the riches to come. I had to trust my father to give me a fair price, but by then I knew that such trust was never misplaced.

When the day came, Dad took all the calves to market – mine included. I could hardly contain my expectation. It was September, and I waited for him with my brother and sisters in the growing darkness of the crossroads as the light went. At last we heard the clip-clop of hoofs and soon the laden trap appeared. Just as the men were paid twice a year, so were we shod and given new clothes. What wonders would it contain? The trap could not accommodate us all and we trotted beside it, questioning Dad on his purchases.

He entered the wide flagged kitchen like Santa Claus with a huge, bulky sack on his back. Out of it, he produced seemingly endless magic. There were lace-up boots for Joseph and a brand new coat for me. Perhaps because it was the day he sold my calf, I remember eight shiny pairs of new wellingtons lined up in the light from the oil lamp. They went down in order of size, beginning with his own and finishing with a tiny red pair for Mary. Aunty Josie, who was staying with us, and our maid, Birdie, got a pair as well. When all the treasures were distributed, he turned to us and handed me two single pound notes and a five pound note. Seven pounds! And I could do what I liked with it. It was a fortune.

The following Saturday, Mauraid and I decided to go by train into Cork City, which was eighteen miles away, in order to spend our earnings. On Friday evening we drew up lists of presents we would purchase for individual members of the family. We went unescorted and a street photographer on whom we spent our first two shillings captured our young, expectant faces in his box camera. Perhaps his practised eye caught the freshness of our exhilaration. The picture, like so much else, is lost.

It was a day to remember. We had a scrumptious lunch at the Kincora Hotel, eating all kinds of exotic foods and finishing up with strawberry wine poured over ice-cream. We bought a hat for Daddy, which was too small, a pink blouse for my mother, a baby doll for Mary for sixpence, a skipping rope and a ball for Joseph, and scented handkerchiefs for Birdie. For gentle Aunty Josie, we bought silvery-looking Rosary beads in a tiny box. I forget what we bought ourselves apart from the joy of spending. We certainly felt we could buy up all Cork.

I know we had four shillings left as we breathlessly returned over the Lee Bridge near the station. In a moment of exuberance, I tipped it into the cap of an old beggar by the wayside. Then, laden with our purchases and replete with happiness, we went into the station. All at once we came back to earth. We had no return tickets and between us we could muster only fivepence ha'penny. We needed about ninepence each.

Unnerved by this sudden calamity, we waited apprehensively for the train. No one questioned us, and we knew that if we reached Mogeely, our father's name would be known to the station master. So it turned out. He let us through, but we had to pull many hundreds of weeds to repay Dad. I never had so much money again until I got my first job, but no money before or since has brought me greater pleasure.

2

Private Family Legends

When we first came to Brookedale in the early spring of 1937, we watched in delight as carpets of primroses and crocuses lit the dark woods around the house with their scented beauty. Every day we made a new discovery until we found a swathe of daffodils dancing across the paddock field. Brookedale had rich productive land, but my mother forbade anyone to plough up the flowers and, as always, my father humoured her. His songs about flowers rang round the house for a while but soon changed to 'Don't Sit Under The Apple Tree (With Anyone Else But Me)' when the orchard burst into blossom.

We were all at an age – under seven at the time – when children have only the haziest memories of early experiences. The optimism of my father must have touched me, for I still remember him step-dancing on the kitchen floor, or telling my mother the whole contents of his current book. We had never heard of television, and Midleton, with its one cinema, was four miles away. My father took his parental responsibilities very seriously and later, as we grew older, he never allowed us to watch a film unless he had first gone and vetted it. Since he rarely had time for such artificial entertainment, I saw just three films before I was fifteen and one of those was the life of Christ.

Free of the compelling attractions of the box, our evenings were full of lively discussions, music and, in due course, homework. My father read every essay we wrote and criticised bluntly and constructively. The next world figured as frequently as this one in our talks and visiting neighbours were automatically drawn in.

'Wouldn't we all get a great land [surprise] if there was nothing at all there when we reach the other side?' asked my father one day. Dead silence descended on the four men around the table. A nervous shifting of chairs indicated shock, and a half-expectation of a thunderbolt from the Almighty. Daddy was always known as 'the Boss' in deference to his status and, I think, obvious integrity.

'Now, Boss,' said Pats Griffin, 'it wouldn't be fair if this was the only world – and the Man Above is surely fair.'

'Besides,' my mother chipped in gently, 'we know there's a good God watching over us – otherwise how do you explain the souls that come back?'

That was the opening for an evening of stories, guaranteed authentic by those who experienced them. All Daddy's side got were warnings – from the Banshee – before someone died. My mother's family, the Hollys, attracted various ghostly visitors. Mammie's most memorable story was about her cousin Father Michael Walsh and his exchanges with a lonely Kerry ghost.

Father Michael spent seven years in Maynooth, where he trained for the priesthood. In those years away from his home in Ballylongford, many old friends and neighbours died. Among them was Pat Murphy who had lived in a small, somewhat isolated cottage outside the town.

This was the same town about which my distinguished cousin Brendan Kennelly wrote *The Crooked Cross*. This title refers to the shape of Ballylongford's streets. Viewed from the top of the church tower, the shape of the town is that of a crooked cross, teeming with life.

Now young Father Michael was a cousin of the Kennellys and our own family. One winter evening, just before Christmas, he was travelling out of town, on his way to the presbytery, when he noticed old Pat Murphy standing somewhat forlornly at the door of his cottage. It was easy to recognise him because he had lost an arm in a farm accident and his loose sleeve was always tucked into his right-hand pocket.

Swift greetings passed between the two men and Father Michael walked whistling on his way. Suddenly, he stopped, the truth dawning on him. That was Pat Murphy back there – dead these three years! Sudden panic lent spurs to his heels and he dashed for home. Feeling a little embarrassed, he told no one until he dropped in for tea with his mother the next day.

'And what did you do, Michael?' inquired his interested mum.

'I ran,' he admitted, adding defensively, 'It's not every day I meet an old acquaintance back from the dead.'

'Now, Michael!' she instructed him. 'Remember you're a priest. Souls come back because they need help. Tonight, if you see him, stop and greet him with a crucifix. Make the sign of the Cross. If he's from God, he'll tell you his troubles. If he's from the devil, he'll vanish before the Cross.'

Michael went off that evening with renewed confidence and, sure enough, there was Pat halfway out of his little front garden. The young priest attempted to address him, but when he looked into the anxious eyes of the long-dead Pat, his courage again failed. He turned and ran.

'Honestly, Mike! I'm ashamed of you,' exclaimed his mother the next day. 'You have a spiritual role and you must be stronger. Now, tonight,' she went on, with a typically Irish solution, 'take a glass of whiskey. It will give you courage!'

That night Pat was waiting by his garden gate – level with the road – when Michael reached him. Raising his crucifix, the priest enquired what in the name of God had brought him back. Pat explained that he had died in debt and he could not rest because he owed eleven pounds seventeen shillings and fourpence in one of Bally-longford's paper shops.

Michael was relieved and gently assured Pat that he would pay his debts next day and, henceforth, he could rest in peace. Early next morning, having told no one of his experience, Michael was waiting outside the paper shop when it opened. To his surprise he found the ownership had changed hands. A young married couple, unknown to him, were running it.

'Did Pat Murphy ever deal here?' he inquired.

The young owner shook her head.

'Do you keep a record of old debts?'

'Not from before our time,' she answered.

Nonplussed that the matter seemed to be more complicated than he had expected, Michael began to wonder if he had somehow hallucinated and imagined the whole thing. He thanked them and began to leave. As he opened the street door a very ancient lady, wrinkled as a walnut, came out of the shop's living quarters.

'Did I hear Pat Murphy's name?' she quavered.

'Yes,' said Michael, eagerly. 'Did you know him?'

'Indeed I did . . . and he died owing us money.'

'Do you know how much?' asked Michael, hopefully.

The old lady, a great-aunt of the present owners, reached for a dusty old ledger and turned to the Ms. 'There!' she asserted triumphantly. 'Eleven pounds seventeen shillings and fourpence.'

Michael paid and went up to the church. Within half an hour, he was called to minister to a dying woman. It was the old great-aunt and she passed peacefully away as he anointed her. It would appear that her work on earth was finished once her excellent memory had succoured the soul of Pat. For his part, he was never seen again.

Though . . . my English husband has informed me since that *his* father had once told him about a Church of England vicar being bothered by a Kerry ghost. The ghost declared he couldn't rest in eternity because he owed the curious sum of eleven pounds seventeen shillings and fourpence to a curate in the parish of Ballylongford. Surely a coincidence! It couldn't have been Pat!

My own experience of supernatural visitations was a bit confusing. After my mother's death, I married an Englishman and took him home to Brookedale, which was so diminished by her loss that it was scarcely recognisable. One evening, while visiting Barry's Pub in Midleton, a young intense IRA supporter took me aside and asked, a shade fiercely, if my new husband had any drop of Irish blood in him. Regretfully, I had to deny this asset and the man, who owed me some loyalty since he'd once worked for my father, urged me to keep quiet about my husband's Englishness while we were at home. It was the time of the Troubles in Northern Ireland.

Back in Brookedale that night I was restless and a bit apprehensive. About 4 a.m. the sound of stealthy tramping round the house roused me to full alertness. Images of women tarred and feathered ran through my mind. Quietly, I left my sleeping husband's side, took a coat of Mother's, which still hung behind the kitchen door, seized an old shotgun held together with wire and walked out to confront my visitors.

Enormous shadows emerged from the trees. As I lined up my

trembling gun on one of them, a loud bellow filled the night. Sixteen straying cows tramped down the avenue and back to the market road. Behind them, I fell automatically into the encouraging noises of my early childhood.

A startled 'God protect us all!' was suddenly and explosively uttered beside me. I heard a scramble of feet slipping on loose stones – and a neighbour I'd known for years retreated quickly into the gloom.

'Paddy?' I exclaimed, just recognising him. 'What are you doing here?'

'O God! Is that you, Kathleen?' he asked weakly. 'I thought you were your mother's ghost.' Of such misunderstandings are legends made.

3
Matchmaking and Other Problems

I suppose if I were asked to summarise the vital elements in our lives at Brookedale I would settle for the farm animals – the horses, the cattle, the poultry and the greyhounds. Before tractors replaced their ancient labour, every farm near us had three or four horses. Two of ours were workers – great big friendly patient animals, who pulled the plough and hay float and became so reliable and valuable that they were regarded as part of the family. A lifespan of twenty-five years or more was normal. We had one brood mare called Peg and her son Paddy, who was born on the same day as my sister Mary. There was always a special bond between them. Our third horse was a high-stepping colt called Blackbird. He could do light farm work, like harrowing, but his main role was to pull the trap when the whole family went to Mass or into town. It was a real milestone when we bought a new horse.

As we grew more prosperous, my father sought a better breed for the trap. In the 1940s and, indeed, most of the 1950s, farmers paid their men twice a year, at harvest time and in the autumn, when the yearling calves were big enough for sale. Thirty shillings to two pounds a week was the average wage for a farm labourer. In our case, we had the added attraction of a tiny cottage on the grounds where a man could stay rent-free with his wife and family. He also received eggs and milk from the farm, and wood for the fire. Occasionally, my mother sent over a fresh chicken as well, especially if there was a new baby or illness in the family.

Every weekend, Jack or Jim was also given half a crown and with this they could go to a dance, get drunk or play cards. In the light of this, it's easy to appreciate the sum of £120, which my father once paid for a well-bred filly. He bought her at Midleton Fair and came home with her in triumph. She was stabled immediately, and after supper, we all trooped down to see her. She was called Marina and her chestnut coat glowed in the setting sun.

However, before we could exclaim at her good looks, we heard it – a sound like a nail in her coffin. A harsh, rasping cough emanated from the stable as the new horse, doped for sale, gradually revealed her broken-winded condition. Whatever chemical had perked up her heart for the sale was the equivalent of an overdose. She hadn't the strength to survive it.

We could ill afford to lose such a valuable animal or the money Dad had been tricked into spending on her. I remember we went back inside and said the family Rosary, trying to accept God's will. I heard Daddy say gallantly to my mother, 'I know this is a setback, but I can survive anything while I have you and the children.'

He was particularly hard hit by the dishonesty of the deal. He was scrupulously honest himself and I'd known him cycle four miles to repay sixpence he had inadvertently collected in a card game. Prompt payment of debts and an absolute adherence to his promises were the twin sources of his self-respect. As children we often tried to manoeuvre him into distracted agreement to some favour we wanted. If he gave his word, we knew nothing could make him break it. He often said, 'A promise made is a debt unpaid.'

Once, when I told him that on a bus journey, the conductor had failed to collect my fare, he sent me back to wait for the next bus an hour later so that I could hand in the twopence that very day.

Although our prayers for the dying horse were not answered favourably that night, my mother claimed the Good Lord had been listening and sent us kindness in another way. In the very hour Marina died, a distant relative of ours came in out of the night. He was Jim Sullivan and he had travelled from Athea in County Limerick in search of a job. He was then about twenty-seven and, as it happened, we needed him. For the next few years, Jim was friend, companion and a very hard worker. He did not go to the lodge but slept in the house – kindly, easy-going Jim, as obliging as another son. He became part of our childhood.

He had a deep voice and a deeper roar. Sometimes he baby-sat when my parents went out and I remember at first being quite nervous of his strict regulations. With a child's instinctive understanding that his bark was worse than his bite, I climbed up on his knee, put my head on his heart and, from this secure perch, I listened to him bellow at the others when their high spirits threatened to get out of hand. He and I were friends from that initial introduction.

Jim, of course, was eminently marriageable, but he managed to survive the enthusiastic blandishments of optimistic mothers and even my father's match-making plans. However, he entered readily into Dad's schemes for other likely young men. The two of them, Jim and Dad, decided it was high time a forty-year-old 'boy' from a local farm met a suitable wife.

Jim undertook to interview the lady, Katie Connors, a plain, rather plump girl of uncertain age, and make her aware of the advantages of marrying Billy Kelly. She expressed faint interest and cautiously agreed to see him. For several evenings, Jim and Daddy coached Billy in the way to conduct himself.

'Right, let Jim be the girl,' said my father. 'Now, come in, Billy, and salute her.'

We children watched the rehearsal through the keyhole and a crack in the hall door.

Billy came in from the yard and said nervously, 'God bless all here.' That was a traditional salutation in Ireland at the time.

'And you too, sir,' responded Jim, in a falsetto voice. Silence followed. Billy stood uncertainly.

'Take off your cap,' hissed my father. Billy snatched it off and turned a complete circle at least twice as he looked for an inoffensive place to put it. Finally he stuffed it into his pocket and sidled closer.

'Please take a seat,' said Jim, reaching for a cup of tea. As Billy sat, the cap fell out of his pocket and on to the tea, which splashed all over Jim's hand. The party broke up in raucous merriment.

After several sessions, Billy was declared ready. Polite nothings didn't exactly trip off his tongue but he was *au fait* with a minimum of safe topics. How was her health? Did she go to the ten o'clock Mass in Mogeely? Did she like the parish priest?

Billy was warned not to mention his own headaches or his eighty-year-old father, who grumpily demanded attention twenty-four hours a day. All those others were acceptable subjects, but Billy anguished over the vital approach to the actual proposal.

Daddy advised him to take it easy, to find something to admire in her – her hair, her cups of tea, her tidy home, then say he wished he had such an accomplished lady in his own house. Jim thought he should also bring her a suitable present and perhaps take her for a walk. Above all, he was to ask to see her again.

Finally, the day came. After a final run-through, the pony was tackled to the trap and Dad and Jim escorted Billy home to make himself ready. He would walk alone to Katie's house, but they left him under strict instructions to report back, the moment he had news. The pair of them settled down to play cards and drink Guinness, anxiously awaiting the outcome.

A bare half-hour later, a disconsolate Billy came in the door.

'Hey! What are you doing here already?' they asked in chorus.

'She threw me out – that's why!' said Billy, bitterly. 'She just threw me out.'

'Hold on,' interrupted Dad. 'Start at the beginning – step by step – and tell us what happened.'

'Well!' revealed the outraged Billy, 'You know, I did as you said. I dressed up – I left my cap at home – I brought her a half-stone of potatoes in the red bag [suppressed expletive from my father] and I thought it best to be honest and straightforward from the start. "You know me, Katie," I said. "I'm forty-one. How old are you?"'

'*What?*' exclaimed the two together, 'You bloody eejit! You asked the girl her *age?* Ach! You're finished there. Don't you know anything about women? You *never* mention their ages – sensitive issue, boy! You'll have to forget her now. I suppose we'll have to look around for another one for you.'

Forget her, Billy did. As far as I know he never parted with another potato and twenty-one years later he was still unwed, for the two disheartened matchmakers never tried again – for him, anyway.

After five or six years with us, Jim left at last for America, seeking his fortune and a family of his own. We all cried after him – and my mother got up at 5 a.m. to cook him a final breakfast. He too was apprehensive about the future. I sneaked down to say goodbye and watched him for the last time as he ran his hands through his black wavy hair.

'Will you be gone long, Jim?' asked my mother.

'"Maybe for years and maybe for ever,"' he quoted softly. His wonderful success and the lovely, brilliant family he reared in Chicago are another story. As a role model, Jim had many qualities that helped to enrich a little girl's life, like an irrepressible sense of fun and a great gift for storytelling – but in retrospect, and in the light of the many men I've met since, I think it is his innocence I recall best.

4
The Dogs of War – and the Dogs of Brookedale

The forties were the best of times and the worst of times. For us in neutral Ireland, they were the best, but I know now that in war-torn Europe, the 'worst' is quite inadequate to describe the living hell that swallowed so many innocents.

The Second World War touched only the fringes of our lives. Britain's demand for bacon, beef and milk encouraged sales and made some farmers fairly prosperous. Ireland could import no food so we had to be self-sufficient and our government imposed some basic rationing. All the war songs were imported and altered to suit our national psychology. Thus we had:

> Bless 'em all, bless 'em all,
> The long and the short and the tall:
> Bless De Valera and Sean McEntee,
> They gave us brown bread and a half-ounce of tea.
> Bless 'em all, bless 'em all,
> Themselves aren't rationed at all –
> They're bringing starvation,
> To our little nation,
> So cheer up St Vincent de Paul!

Uncle Frank was a creamery manager in Mountcollins, County Kerry. Early on in the war, he made a contract with United Dairies in London to supply milk for the duration. Even when United Dairies were unable to pay him at one stage, he continued to supply the milk. My dad called it a 'master-stroke of business'. United Dairies showed their appreciation in due course and, ever after, took all the milk and butter he could produce.

What shortages there were brought out a whole tribe of enthusiastic tinkers, who frequently filled our ears with tales of hardship. My mother was invariably kind to them. When the war started, Dad was fortunate enough to obtain a chest of Ceylon tea. It contained 144 pounds of the precious stuff and, carefully managed, it lasted right through to 1945. Secretly, however, I reduced it by giving away generous helpings to the tinker who told the sorriest tale. My mother gave them clothes, bread and bacon – those we had in abundance – but she never gave them tea. So while she comforted them at one door, I went out of the other to offer them handfuls of the brown leaves. No one could understand why they kept turning up. My aunt said they left a private mark on the gate to alert each other, and I spent hours crawling among tree roots trying to find it.

My parents strongly believed in sharing with those in need and my dad told frequent stories of the desperation of the starving people during the famine when English landlords exacted their 'rack-rents'. One such account was of a hungry man at the back door of a visiting landlord's great house.

'Help me,' he begged, 'I'm eating the grass with the hunger.'

'My good man,' the lady of the house is reported to have said. 'Go around to the front. There's much better grass there.'

Apart from begging, the tinkers – nowadays called Travellers – also traded in dogs and ponies. Half a dozen collies ran with them and were available on a *quid pro quo* basis to any farmer who wanted one. The tinkers were also willing to take away less promising pups that drove cows into the quarry. In a way they were like an unofficial Battersea Dogs Home before that institution became world-famous. My father did regular business with them and we grew up with a minimum of three dogs and five cats. Once, all the cats had kittens together, and for a brief period we had twenty-seven kittens scurrying about above the stables. I remember standing with my mother while one fussy mother-cat carried each of her kittens, in her mouth, up a long ladder to a new resting place in the hay-barn.

'How did God ever think of them?' asked my mother, wonderingly, absorbed in the perfect maternal instincts of the little cat.

One of our dogs, Sam, was a positive star. He seemed to understand every nod and wink my father gave him. When ordered to 'die for Ireland', he would stretch himself instantly on the ground with his eyes shut and his tail still. Sam was not born in Brookedale, however, nor did he come from the tinkers. Like many others, he wandered in one morning, was hugged and fed, and after that he simply refused to go away. For six months, no one claimed him and he became my father's shadow. He had only one unflattering habit. When Daddy sang, Sam raised his own lugubrious voice in loud lamentation. It embarrassed my father and was a source of limitless hilarity to the rest of us. I think this was one reason why he slept in the barn.

After six months, we were shattered to learn that an East Cork man was claiming him and, indeed, needed him to control his vast herds. Sadly, we watched Sam depart, looking cowed and reproachful. He was taken by car to his old home about thirty miles away.

There was no cheerful whistle from Dad as he laced his shoes the next morning, but when he opened the door there was Sam, exhausted and mud-spattered, but triumphantly back! Two days later the East Cork man collected him again, and none of us cared for we knew Sam would return – and so he did. After that, his owners tied him up at the back of their garage until they needed him.

One night one of their sons forgot about Sam being there, and reversed the car on top of him. He was so crushed and bleeding that they concluded he was dead and threw out his body onto a rubbish dump. We knew nothing about that at the time.

About eleven days later, we heard a faint scratching at the kitchen door. There lay Sam, thin and starved as we'd never known him. He had crawled on his stomach across country roads and muddy fields to reach us. His back was broken in three places and his ribcage was cracked. Only his brave heart had kept him going. My father and Jim spent the morning putting splints where they could, while my mother let Sam lick warm milk off her fingers. He took about six months to recover, and for the next twelve years of his life, he had three knobbly lumps on his spine. No one ever came for him again – and we would not have given him up if they had. He was the lord of the yard: every dog and cat deferred to him and learned from him, and increasingly we loved him.

Sam wasn't the only interesting dog we owned. We also had a small black mongrel called Shep. Shep was the only dog I've ever met who could definitely smile. The smile was a bit artful and deceitful. In fact, my father also called him 'Higgins' because that smile reminded him of a sneaky, somewhat underhand tax inspector he disliked. Shep would eat the chickens' new-laid eggs and smile. He would steal meat off the table and smile. It was a most unnerving sight, almost as if there was a human mind behind it, but we forgave his small delinquencies and kept him.

I remember Jimmy Hennessey coming into the yard with his own dog. Now Jimmy was another local man 'without guile'. He loved children and we all gathered round him when he arrived. In my Ireland, the pace of life was slow. Everyone seemed to have time for everyone else and Jimmy was no exception. When our pack of dogs, Sam and Shep among them, descended on Jimmy's dog to begin a thorough investigation, I heard my brother's piping voice ask, 'Jimmy, why are our dogs sniffing round your dog?'

'Now that's an easy one,' Jimmy answered. 'Sit down here and I'll tell you all about it.'

Full of curiosity and anticipating a story, we four sat around on logs and listened intently.

'You know God made the world,' he began. We nodded earnestly. 'Well, at the beginning of Creation, God was dishing out all the right parts to the various animals. That is why some have long silky ears, some have fluffy coats and some short legs. As a result of God's care, every animal ended up with the right eyes, teeth and paws. Well, it was near the end of the sixth day when God got around to the dogs. He was getting a bit tired and looking forward to his day of rest. He had nearly finished them and had just one more part to dish out. As I said, he was a bit weary, so he gathered all the parts into one big heap, called the nearly finished dogs together, and said, "Here, for my sake, will you sort out your own arses?" Now, naturally there was a mad scramble and many mistakes were made. That is why, for ever more, every dog you ever meet is searching hard, trying to find his own bottom.'

*

Nearly every family in the district had a greyhound or two and they were an integral part of our lives in Brookedale. They held a special fascination because there was always the chance, no matter how remote, that one of them would be a winner.

My father and his brother Frank spent hours discussing races and dogs with local owners. The achievements of famous dogs like Mick the Miller and, closer to home, Dick's Express were embellished with every telling. Dick's Express was owned by a distant cousin, Jack Mackessey, who was a shrewd judge of greyhounds and went almost into ecstasy when one of his many dogs won.

As Uncle Frank lived in Kerry, he instructed my father to look out for a promising greyhound pup for him. We had at one time a silky-looking bitch called Brookedale Girl. She made reasonable time at the track but broke no records. She was given almost as much care as a child. She was fed on chicken, eggs, vitamins and cod-liver oil. Her pet name was Breeze and she followed us everywhere in the summer holidays. In particular, she liked to accompany us to the river that bordered our land. Breeze was considered far too valuable and too delicately bred to splash with us in the waters. One of us always stayed on the bank to keep a grip on her. Once, it was our friend, Maudie Griffin, who had this boring task. She sat and hugged her knees while we played and swam, stroking the dog's head. It was a warm day, and in a moment of drowsy abstraction, she let slip her hold on the collar. Breeze leaped instantly into the fast-flowing river.

Maudie was a delicate only child, aged about eleven at the time. Her mother was inclined to be over-protective and we had been warned not to let her anywhere near the cold water. It had made her the perfect choice to hold the dog. In her endeavours to save Breeze however, the shrieking Maudie fell headlong into the flood. We were appalled at her shivering state as we rushed to drag her out. Luckily, it was a hot sunny day and we solved the problem by telling her to strip off and we would soon get her clothes dry. The plan worked fairly well. When her dress was wearable, she took off her wet knickers and my brother Joseph elected to sit on them to dry them out.

In the midst of all this pandemonium, we forgot all about Breeze. When we remembered to look for her, she was out of the water, on the other side of the river. She, too, was dripping and shivering. We dared not let her repeat the journey back alone and I was sent across to carry her over. Trying to hold the slippery dog high in the air, I wandered a little off course and found myself, unable to swim, up to my armpits in fast-running water. I still remember the terror of that moment and my dread of snarling otters that might attack my toes. The others were distractedly grabbing sandwiches and orangeade. Only Joseph, from his lonely vigil on the knickers, saw my predicament, but he had to stick to his appointed task, in a manner of speaking.

I recall in particular my moment of truth. The water swirled fiercely around me and the earth and sky appeared to be moving too. I had to decide which of us mattered most to my father: Breeze or myself? And I knew, as I threw the whimpering dog from me, that I did. Naturally, Breeze swam ahead of me, better in the water than I was. When she was out again, we all dried her frantically. She did not catch cold but neither did she make our fortunes. She was kept for breeding and, in due course, she had five affectionate pups. It was neither fast women nor slow horses that took my father's money: it was partly slow greyhounds.

True to his promise, Dad eventually chose a strong, lively brindle pup for his brother Frank. He earmarked the most likely pup in the litter for himself and kept the next best for Frank. These two greyhounds grew up in Brookedale until the time came for them to go to the track. Uncle Frank took his away and employed a top-class trainer to prepare him for racing.

In due time, hundreds of miles apart, they were both sent for trials. Our dog competed against five other hopefuls and barely qualified. One of the other dogs must have brought an infection to the track. Of the six that ran that evening, three died the next day and ours never fully recovered. Uncle Frank's dog broke all records. He entered the greyhound history books as Flaming King. He ran and won in London's White City and was eventually sold in America for thousands of pounds. A song was written about him called 'Moran's Flaming King'. My father never begrudged Uncle Frank his success with Flaming King, though he teased him for years about the percentage of profits he reckoned Frank owed him. I never go back to Brookedale now without going to the dogs in Youghal.

5
Keeping the Faith

Any recapitulation of an Irish childhood would be incomplete without stressing the natural dimension of spirituality in our lives. In fact, dimension is probably the wrong word, for without any heavy puritanical straitjackets, we grew up to rely on a loving God whose help was always 'nearer than the door'. Our faith was a way of life. Later on, when I met people who were atheists, I tended to feel quite lost. I didn't know how to communicate with these 'half-people', as they appeared to me. It was like stepping off into a vacuum where I had no recognisable terms of reference. How my parents planted the Faith in us, I don't know. They never forced religion on us, but perhaps we adopted their values because we loved them. A teacher at school had a favourite quotation about that:

> What thou lovest, thou becomest,
> Christ – if thou lovest Christ
> And dust if thou lovest dust.

Anyway, they gave us both roots and wings. Turning to God and His Mother for help was as natural as the air we breathed. Of course, like all thinking teenagers, we challenged His very existence as we developed, but none of us lost the faith and each is now trying to pass it on. We never saw prayer as a mere opportunity to ask God for what we wanted. A readiness to please Him with good, unselfish lives was as important as acquiring material things. We didn't expect gratuitous miracles. For example, we knew we had to work hard to pass exams: 'God helps those who help themselves,' was a common household saying, but a readiness to help others too, was taken for granted.

31

'Never demand of God,' my mother often told us. 'He is wiser than you are. What you ask may not be good for you. Trust in His love.'

As a girl, my mother spent six months in America, touring amongst her numerous relatives and visiting places as far north as Niagara Falls in Canada. Her father, Dan Holly, loved the States and he wanted his daughter to experience a wider world before she settled down in Ireland. She was a great storyteller and we were entertained all through childhood with fascinating stories of her exploits over there – so much so that we thought of it as a magical place, flowing with the proverbial 'milk and honey'. While she was in Chicago, she became great friends with a saintly old priest. His story of one of his formative experiences helped to shape her own attitude to God.

In the early years of the twentieth century – about 1920 – Father Rigby had been a young curate in a wild country parish at the foot of the Rockies. One of his parishioners was a widowed lady who had a dearly loved four-year-old son. She was a devout Catholic and Father Rigby developed a true friendship with her. In the mid-1920s, he was ordered by his bishop to go to a new parish where he was badly needed. The parish was several hundreds of miles away in north Canada. The afternoon before he left, a distressed message reached the presbytery that young Sean B., the lady's son, was desperately ill. Father Rigby hurried to the house to bring what comfort he could. As he arrived, the doctor was on the point of leaving. He took Father Rigby aside and told him sadly that the boy had no chance. At best, he might last the night, but he could die at any moment.

Father Rigby was welcomed by the mother, and the neighbours who sat by the child's bedside. He joined them in prayer and, as the slow hours passed, the boy grew visibly weaker. Eventually he fell into unconsciousness. At that point, his mother exploded in anger and grief. God was cruel, she said, and she threatened that if Sean died, she would curse God and never darken the door of a church again. Father Rigby was saddened but understanding of her hysterical outburst. Henceforth, she went on, she would hate God.

The boy was clearly dying when, at about midnight, rapid audible steps approached the house. It was a message from the bishop. A light aircraft was travelling to Ottawa the next morning and the priest was offered a lift. He would be saved four days of arduous travel if he accepted it. Reluctantly, he left the grief-stricken mother with her kindly neighbours and promised prayers that she would survive her ordeal.

It was over twenty years before he was transferred back to the States, and in that time he had received no news of her or her family. As he walked out of New York airport in the early morning, he heard the sound of sobbing. Ahead of him, an elderly woman stumbled along the street, blind to the existence of others as she cried in unknown anguish. Father Rigby stopped and said softly, 'Madam, I am a priest. You seem to be in bad trouble. Is there anything I can do to help you?'

The old lady straightened and looked at him. As she did so, he recognised her. 'Helen!' he said in amazement. 'What new sorrow has befallen you?' She remained silent, obviously not knowing him.

'Don't you remember me?' he went on. 'I was with you the night young Sean died.'

'Well, he didn't die,' she replied harshly, 'but he went to the electric chair this morning!'

We took it for granted that our parents prayed about every event in our lives. The prayers were neither long-winded nor burdensome. Like every other family, we had a regular Rosary with a number of additional prayers called 'the Trimmings'. Far from being dreary or wearying, they involved all of us so personally that they were quite fascinating. It was as though God couldn't remember our exams next day, or the cow about to calve, unless we reminded Him. I remember Jimmy Hennessey, a visitor to the Rosary one night, getting up from his knees as the Trimmings began.

'Not finished yet, Jim,' said Mam.

'I'm not leaving,' he replied. 'I'm just going out to the hall to get a coat for my knees – carry on.'

Throughout my youth, we had a remarkably attractive maid called Birdie Walsh. She and my mother prepared for Christmas all during

Advent, by saying four thousand special prayers in praise of the birth of Jesus. It ran as follows:

> Hail and blessed be the hour and moment in which the Son of God was born, at midnight in Bethlehem, in piercing cold. In that hour, vouchsafe, O my God, to hear my prayer.

They began the four-thousand-prayer marathon early in Advent and reported daily to each other on their progress. My mother also told us beautiful old legends about the big feasts of the Church. On Christmas Eve, she said, as the clocks of the world struck midnight, all the animals, from the elephants in the jungle and the wolves on the plains, to the cows, pigs and horses on the farms, went down on their knees to worship the memory of God-made-man. Furthermore, all the water in the wells turned to wine for a few minutes.

My father brought in a large turnip and scooped a hole in it for a fat red candle, which burned invitingly on a windowsill all night. Mary, as the youngest in the family, lit it and we hoped it would serve as a beacon to any homeless person who might be looking for a room on that holy eve.

Our house was high up on a green hill, and if you looked out over the dark valleys at midnight, you could see the twinkling gleam of candlelight in every neighbouring house. Those soft, friendly lights became for me a symbol of the faith and idealism that united our little community with the rest of Ireland.

Beside the candle there was always a glass of wine and a thick slice of Christmas cake. The kitchen door was left unlocked for this one night in winter, but it was usual to leave it open every night in summer. No one was more pleased than my mother to find someone asleep on the settee when she came down in the morning. It was usually a friend or relative, though it was common practice to find the postman having his breakfast at the kitchen table as well. He usually made the tea and boiled an egg for himself.

I remember one spring through to summer, we had a clean, fat lamb called Lucy, who was hand-reared. She must have been more precocious than the rest of us for she knew about a crisis of identity and even had one herself. She thought she was the cat: she drank milk

34

under the table and made mewing noises for scraps. She appeared in many family photographs and she slept in the barn with Sam. Ever since, I have associated that pet lamb with Easter.

All our seasons had their links with nature. For instance, I sometimes rose about 5 a.m. on Easter Sunday to watch the misty sun come up behind the trees. I was convinced that it would dance briefly on the tree-tops, shedding glorious shimmering light down the glen as it rejoiced in the Resurrection. No pictures I've seen have equalled the pristine beauty of those eager early mornings. The dew glinted on the grass, silent rabbits left their tracks along the hayfields and sleepy birds woke. The mists lifted almost miraculously, as if a giant hand had gathered them into wispy nothingness. Above them, the moving sun rose, majestic as Christ Himself, and I could swear it danced in Easter jubilation. Soon, Daddy sang a song about Easter bonnets, and we all went off to Mass.

On weekdays, we walked the three miles to the 'National School'. Ballintotas was a tiny three-teacher primary school with a headmaster – Mr Collins – and just two lady teachers. I lost all credibility with one of them, little Mrs Fleming, when I put a long-nosed live harvest mouse into one of her indoor shoes one morning. Those teachers were not only our friends but our parents' friends as well. Mrs Brennan, who always arrived in a pony and trap, had two daughters, Bussy and Margot, at the school and they became our lasting childhood companions.

In the autumn term of 1945, into this little Eden came Mrs Fleming's grim replacement. He was young and good-looking and a bit pompous. I will call him Mr Welsh. He invited himself to Sunday lunch occasionally, but my hospitable parents found it difficult to warm to him. He was the first man in my immediate circle to make me conscious that I was growing up. He had a tendency to run his eyes slowly over me in a speculative fashion that made me feel vaguely uncomfortable.

To begin with, he was a reasonable teacher, though he had frightening and unpredictable fits of rage. The cane was used sparingly at the school, but none of us Morans had ever been touched. We put this down to the friendship that existed between my father and Mr Collins. They often had a drink together and discussed our progress and promise. A firm word from Dad was all that was needed to bring us into line.

Of all of us, Joseph was the one who needed encouragement. As the only son, he was the apple of my mother's eye. She had removed him instantly from another school when he was five because a short-tempered teacher had slapped him across the face. He was then given into the care of the motherly Mrs Brennan in Ballintotas. She took as much pride in his progress as my mother herself. Mammie missed the four of us so much that she was known to make delicious fudge, tackle the pony and trap and drive down to Ballintotas – all to have an excuse to see us in the lunch hour.

The September Mr Welsh arrived, Joseph reached the age of nine and said goodbye to Mrs Brennan. He was transferred automatically into the nine-to-eleven-year-old set, who came under Mr Welsh's care.

All went fairly well the first year, though Mr Welsh's explosive temper tantrums grew more alarming and frequent. One morning at Break, he found out that his bicycle tyres were flat and convinced himself that Joseph either knew or was the culprit. A smack with the cane was the normal, if seldom used, punishment. Joseph denied all knowledge of the flat tyres and was ordered to hold out his hands. Wincing, he received six strikes on each hand, but neither cried nor revealed a name to the by then semi-hysterical Mr Welsh. The teacher was further incensed by the boy's determination not to cry. My sister Mary, who witnessed the scene, was sobbing to herself as she watched her brother stand against roaring, red-faced anger.

It became a contest of wills. Mr Welsh decided to make Joseph cry. Hitting him on the legs or the hands again and again, he asked, 'Did that *hurt* you, Moran?'

And Joseph would shake his head and say, 'No, sir.'

Welsh kept on till the poor child's hands swelled up and the teacher himself was exhausted.

The trembling boy never made a sound and afterwards he warned his sister not to mention it at home. As young as she was, Mary knew that my father, the mildest of men, would be capable of near-murder if he were to learn of the attack. Joseph managed to avoid a few sub-sequent family meals until he could hold his knife and fork once more. Later that year, Mr Welsh went completely off his head and died quite young in a mental home.

Despite that awful incident, it was, I think, a good school. In due course, I became a teacher myself, though I never met anyone to match the versatility of Mr Collins. Now, he was a superb storyteller and actor. Most classes in Ballintotas lasted about thirty-five minutes but Irish history had pride of place. To this, he allocated the whole of every Friday afternoon. Surrounded by reference books, he leaped onto a table where he sat cross-legged, like a tailor. He told us stories full of courage, pathos and humour from the days of Brian Boru to the Great Famine. He picked up and discarded reference books with unrestrained enthusiasm. He read excerpts, sang famous songs and recited poetry in his rich, deep voice. I well remember his amusement when he was describing a charge of pike-men and he asked if we could draw a pike. Every hand shot up. We were, after all, from a farming community. I reached the blackboard first and proudly drew a quite creditable pitchfork.

'A fearsome weapon indeed, Kate,' he laughed, 'but a pike is a wicked, bladed thing.' I retired, deflated.

It was from him I learned my love of poetry. I recall vividly his declamation of 'The Heroine of Ross':

> And her voice rang o'er the clamour,
> Like a trumpet o'er the sea,
> 'Who so dares to die for Ireland,
> Let him come and follow me.'

Mr Collins played on our emotions like a violinist, but he must have had his own integrity, for I think we ended up reasonably balanced. In the last year at school, we had a public examination, but each year we also had a small, searching test. We were visited by a diocesan priest to find out the extent of our religious knowledge. In preparation for this, we tended to learn the Catechism off by heart. He had only to mention the theme of a parable and we launched instantly into the full story, including every stop and comma, like a released spring.

One rather inflexible priest always began with Question 1 in the Catechism and worked his way through in the exact order, all round the class. I know of an ill-prepared teacher who took advantage of this predictability by teaching each pupil only one answer. If they stood in the order in which the questions were asked, all would be well. Of course, no one was allowed to be late or absent that day, or the whole ploy would be thrown out of kilter. The first question was 'When should you pray?' and number-one pupil had memorised the answer. Number two question, 'Why did God make you?' came next and was duly learned. When they were all word perfect in their answers, His Reverence appeared. Whether it was the genial atmosphere, or his welcoming cup of tea, but for the first time in his life the priest changed his routine. Maybe he just wanted to put these country children at their ease with a little familiar small-talk. He turned to the first girl, whose nerves were stretched to breaking point with expectation.

'Well, my dear,' he inquired amiably, 'when do you milk the cows?'

She came to with a jerk and in a high squeaky voice reeled off the astonishing answer: 'In the morning, in the evening, before and after meals and in all dangers, temptations and afflictions.'

Mr Collins belonged to a vanishing breed of headmasters. He and the parish priest were trusted to have encyclopaedic knowledge of all legalities. At least twice a week, a harassed farmer arrived to see the 'master' about his tax demands, his land-clearance grants or the making of his will. We were given work to do and Mr Collins went patiently through the tangle of papers. He dealt with all these affairs in confidence and was never known to mention other people's private business. Goldsmith's master in 'The Deserted Village' describes him very well – 'And still they gazed, and still the wonder grew, that one small head could carry all he knew' – except we never laughed at his jokes with 'counterfeited glee'. He was genuinely funny and pitched his humour at our level. Whenever we failed to catch on, he might be heard to murmur something about 'wasting sweetness on the desert air'. It was from him we learned to appreciate Gray's 'Elegy':

> Full many a gem of purest ray serene,
> The dark unfathomed caves of ocean bear:
> Full many a flower is born to blush unseen
> And waste its sweetness on the desert air.

At about the age of twelve, each of us left the delightful intimacy of Ballintotas School to go to the nuns or the brothers in Midleton. So began our higher education ...

6
Teenagers

I feel enormous sympathy for today's teenagers, especially our city youngsters, deprived so early of the experience of being young, in a drug-oriented society, with many more broken homes and exposure to an amoral culture. We were protected from the kinds of exploitation and insecurity that are so commonplace today. We had never even heard of teenagers. I think the word came from America in the fifties. The amalgam of raw, smouldering resentment and unhappiness that characterises so many modern teenagers was simply unknown to us. As for a crisis of identity, the only crisis we ever came across was the urgent need of our parents to identify which bills had to be paid first. 'Peer groups', however, we did know about. Were they not the odd-job men who repaired the piers at the entrance of people's houses?

Our teen years were marked only by extra responsibility around the farm. For instance, I learned how to milk a cow, and instead of merely bringing food out to the men in the fields at harvest time, we began to give a hand with the golden stooks that lined the hillsides. However, our contributions were limited to holidays, for my mother was determined that we should be educated. Daily, my older sister Mauraid and I cycled the four miles to Midleton where the Presentation Sisters taught us.

I have never understood why the products of some Catholic schools go out of their way to denigrate their teachers. Generally speaking, we liked ours. The priests were the sons and brothers of local people, part of a long tradition of loyalty and bravery when Ireland was occupied by the British. The nuns may have had some quaint customs, but they came from families very much like our own. They had left their relations, full

of youthful idealism and generosity. In their green years, they plighted
their troth with God, often offering Him more gifts of nature and Grace
than the rest of us. My memories may lend those years a veil of flippancy, but in fact I survived my time at the convent school with my
illusions intact and my regard for the nuns undiminished. I've met many
university professors since then, some of them world authorities, but our
scholarly Presentation nuns would have found a place among them easily. We laughed and giggled at their inflexible attitudes and their regard
for established proprieties but, in retrospect, I agree wholeheartedly
with an American girl's comment: 'They were the grandest body of
ladies God had drafted on His side.'

In academic subjects, our foundations were broad. We spent so much
time learning by heart and making notes that we had no time for a crisis
of any sort, even if we had known what it was. At that time, music was
one of the few fringe subjects they offered. The genuine ability to master
a musical instrument was encouraged. Needlework, too, was taught to a
high standard. In each year, a complete article of clothing had to be finished in its entirety. I remember beginning with a pair of voluminous
knickers – always decently referred to as 'the garment'. The word itself
was never uttered. I still recall a friendly visiting parish priest inquiring
what we were making. Blushing to the ears, we murmured, 'A *garment*,
Father,' and pushed the shapeless articles out of sight.

Towards the end of the 1940s, an educational revolution took place
in our convent school. Physical education was introduced – not during
the school day, of course: that would have been sheer frivolity. No, every
Saturday morning, we assembled in the playground. A muscular young
man (another innovation) led us all in swift, orderly leaps and bounds,
while one of the Sisters kept a gimlet eye on both him and us. We jumped
and stretched and ran at his command in full uniform – gymslips and
blouses – and then we filed back sedately to our classrooms. Showing
one's legs in shorts was regarded as really fast behaviour.

In that haven of good old-fashioned values, we did receive some sex
education. A tiny, ancient nun, whom we irreverently called 'Mick',
duly contributed this gem to the curriculum, one day each summer.
Her full name was Mother St Michael and she drifted around like a
wraith among the senior girls, moving from group to group while we

chatted in the warm sunshine. She had a slight lisp, so one had to listen carefully. When our turn came for enlightenment, she said softly, 'Always remembah, girls, loff-making should be knightly.'

There followed an astonished pause, then . . .

'Observe the K,' and she melted away. That was it! The subject was never referred to again.

The nuns had their own established ways of imposing discipline. Inattention was dealt with by exclusion from the lesson and the culprit was sent to stand where she could be seen through a glass partition by at least three classrooms. Behaviour that was regarded as outrageous, such as answering a teacher back, was so rare that the Reverend Mother was called in to adjudicate. She arrived in a swirl of black skirts, flying veils and accompanied by the noisy clinking of large Rosary beads. She fixed the offender with a sad, disapproving eye while the transgressions were listed. Loud tuts of disapproval greeted each new revelation. Then the girl was reminded that this was a fee-paying school and asked how she could square the waste of her parents' money with her conscience. What was she contributing with her lazy, feckless attitude? Finally, if she showed no proper sense of repentance, the Holy Water was sent for and she was liberally sprinkled with it, while the Reverend Mother walked all round her, muttering half-audible prayers. St Jude, the patron saint of hopeless cases, figured prominently in these. After all that, pupils rarely stepped out of line.

There was a lovely Czechoslovakian girl in our class. She was a blue-eyed golden creature of such grace and daintiness that even her unflattering school uniform looked fashionable. Her father managed a model farm near Midleton. Her name was Sonya Navratil and her wealthy, cultured family horrified the neighbourhood with the prominent display of an oil painting of their son, Alan, in their front hall. It was a full-length portrait of a naked young man, aged about five!

'There he was, without a stitch on him!' said the narrow and strait-laced Mrs Keane, primly. Many of the locals who saw it came away quiet and bemused at such shamelessness. At school, Mr Navratil's beautiful daughter found the shackles of conventual discipline hard to accept. When we were all preparing for Confirmation, we came to the section on 'the pledge'. A vow of total abstinence from alcohol up to the age of twenty-five! I must admit I thought it was an essential part of the sacrament and I was a little surprised when a kindly nun explained that the oath was quite voluntary. We all agreed to take it even so, to protect ourselves in our vulnerable years from the demon drink. Ever since I first heard, from Mr Collins, of Father Murphy from Old Kilcormack who 'rushed up the hill with his warning cry', I thought he was raising the alarm about Guinness. Then, too, we heard of the reformed alcoholic, Matt Talbot, and admired his lonely fight for self-control.

The next time we gathered in class, Sonya put up her hand and announced that she wouldn't take the pledge. We were astounded and not a little shocked.

'Not taking the pledge, Sonya?' inquired Sister, regretfully, as if she were already slipping down the black road to perdition. 'But why? Why, my dear?'

'Because,' said Sonya, 'I want to drink cocktails at Christmas.'

Curiosity jostled with surprise in our minds at this daring stand. Cocktails! What kind of brew was this? None of us were allowed anything stronger than ginger wine at Christmas. I suppose every household was told of the episode that evening, and the general opinion seemed to be that such behaviour was only to be expected from a home that displayed oil paintings of naked little boys. Sonya's stature, however, rocketed among her peers, who both loved and admired her.

While still in her teens, Sonya made a disastrous early marriage when she eloped with a handsome but illiterate stableboy. Five years later, she returned from penury to her parents' house, accompanied by two small sons. Her mother opened her loving arms to them all. The once handsome husband had turned into a drunken slob and slunk away out of their lives.

Her father took them all to America, where Sonya became a celebrated Washington hostess. When news of all that filtered back, the nuns remembered she had been the one who wouldn't take the pledge. Yet who we are in our teens, is not all we become.

7
Lady Luck

My dad always maintained that there are three facets to a man's life which encompass him completely – and in any two of which he must find contentment in order to be happy. They are: his family (that is, his love life), his job and his hobby. Very few get all three right, but even one gives him a chance of satisfaction and perhaps compensation for the other two. My father always claimed that he belonged to the rare breed who had all three right. He loved my mother and was intrigued and stimulated by his children, who in turn regarded him with unwavering affection. He enjoyed being a farmer, even when the work was hard and relentlessly demanding. Finally, he loved his music and playing cards with friends.

He was particularly good at whist and often won a prize. After winning three successive matches and each time being awarded a scrawny chicken that looked as though it would die of malnutrition, he was jubilant one Christmas when he learned that he'd won a turkey. I remember him telling my mother, herself knee-deep in turkeys with fifty-three gorgeous and glossy market-ready birds, that he was to go the next morning to pick up his prize.

He brought the turkey hen home in a basket attached to his bicycle and released her in the yard. We dutifully tramped out to admire this superior addition. There she was, huddled in a corner, lame of leg and blind in one eye. The enormous turkey cock took an instant dislike to her. If Sam, exercising some primitive doggie instinct for protection, hadn't championed her so vigorously, she'd have been pecked to death. Dad was a bit crestfallen at our jeers and kept his next piece of luck to himself for a while.

This time he didn't win anything, but he got the opportunity of a lifetime to buy a flock of thirty sheep at give-away prices. They came from a part of Ireland where there was little grazing and some steep rocky mountains. For some time Dad had wanted sheep for Brooke-dale, to follow the cows and horses. When in 1941 he was offered that splendid bargain – half a crown a sheep – he jumped at the chance. They arrived at Mogeely station and Dad and Jim Sullivan drove them home. I met them at the gates and thought they were the liveliest, most nimble-footed sheep I'd ever seen. They seemed inclined to follow secret paths invisible to the dog and to ourselves, more like mountain goats than sheep. The first evening they were put into the lawn field, and they were gone in the morning.

Thus it began. They broke out or jumped over any fence or gate erected to stop them. They seemed to scent fields of cabbages three miles away and set off at a gallop to find them. In passing, they ate the bark of young trees, swallowed every daffodil that bloomed before them, and trampled and destroyed what they didn't eat. They were like vultures, and within a week we were facing a barrage of complaint from our hitherto good-natured neighbours. One man swore he found a couple of them climbing his apple trees. (In fact, they were on the wide wall beside his orchard, reaching hungrily for his apples.)

The normal tenor of our lives was utterly disrupted by them. When we went to school and pupils regaled our teachers with the highlights of the previous evening, we began to hear with monotonous regularity, 'And, Miss, Moran's sheep broke into our turnips!'

'Miss! Moran's sheep ate half our cabbages.'

We were ashamed and mortified. Dad couldn't wait for us to arrive home so he could send us out again in search of the errant sheep. Even Mauraid, who never really mastered the art of riding, was hijacked to search for them. There was no way she was going to walk four or five miles so she decided to take Dandy, a small Welsh pony about as do-cile as a child. Joseph and I took Billy and Paddy and set off out to scour the countryside.

'Hey! Give me a hand up!' cried Mauraid. We airily assured her that we'd no time, and if she lined Dandy up beside a wall, she could soon slide across to his back.

Off we went, each taking a different road. At the crossroads, I turned to look back and saw Mauraid from her position on the high wall, placing the tip of her foot gingerly against Dandy's side. The patient animal bore one touch, but when she tried to slide across, her nervousness communicated itself and he moved away from the wall at the critical moment. She fell with a shriek to the ground between the horse and the wall. Three times I saw her get up gamely and try again, but as she sprawled in a heap for the third time, I galloped away, chuckling unsympathetically to myself.

That evening was the last straw for Dad. The following Friday was Fair Day in Midleton and he marched the entire flock of wild, scatter-brained sheep to market and sold them with more relief than regret. At his next whist drive, he came first again and was given a choice of prizes. On my mother's orders he avoided all half-dead livestock and came home instead with a bottle of poteen.

8

The Shaping of Early Loyalties

In our household, we grew up with a love of Ireland and tales of the Old IRA's exploits during the War of Independence as part of the warp and weft of our lives. As a girl in Ballylongford, my mother, sensitive and gentle as she undoubtedly was, carried messages for Irish troops as part of her work for the Cumman na mBan (Women's Corps). She was awarded a medal for her services by a grateful Irish government in 1945.

She remembered a hail of bullets, from a lorryload of 'Black and Tans',[2] kicking up the road around her and frightening the horse that drew her trap from Ballylongford. Unable to control the terrified animal, she jumped out and pulled the horse towards a gate to get him off the road. The sight of her fear amused the soldiers and they risked closer and closer bullets round her feet. A sergeant, more sober than his men, probably saved her life. He suddenly tired of the game, ordered the driver to move on and left the trembling girl to soothe her horse and return home.

She'd had reason to be afraid. Only a month before, on that very road, her cousin Eddie Carmody, an only son, was shot as he walked home with two friends. When the firing began (and it always seemed to be haphazard and unpredictable, depending on the mood of the Tans), the three young men ran. The other two got far enough away

---

2 Name given to the British Auxiliary troops, sent to support the RIC (Irish police) who had been under attack since the Easter Rising of 1916. Their black and tan uniform reminded the people of a famous pack of hounds of the same name.

to hide and observe, but Eddie was injured in the leg by a stray bullet. Badly frightened, he scrambled over a fence and dived for cover.

He probably thought he was safe and, indeed, he almost was. The Tans, who didn't even know the youngster's name, were about to give up the search, when one of them saw the bloody trail from his leg wound. Triumphantly, like a pack on heat, they followed it in noisy, drunken elation. They found Eddie, by then weak and almost unconscious. He was dragged out and, without even the semblance of a trial, propped against a fence and shot. His body had seven bullet holes in it.

I remember my mother, some thirty years later, stopping by the plaque on the roadside erected in his memory and telling me that the shadow of his blood lay on the ground for ten years. I recall, with a shiver, looking very carefully, and imagining that I, too, could see the tragic final evidence of the young man's life.

Then there was Mick Mack. He was a terror to the Black and Tans. My mother and Aunty Josie, the maiden aunt who lived with us, regaled us with tales of his exploits. Aunty Josie's face lit up with unaccustomed humour when she told of his daredevil escapades and hair-raising feats while the Black and Tans chased him all over north Kerry. Once he was hidden under a dining-table, which had a floor-length cover, while a dozen soldiers searched the house and the women of the household stood around looking suitably aggrieved at the intrusion. Eventually, this folk-hero got away to America and we all felt, even a generation later, that north Kerry was a duller place without him.

Trigger-happy – most certainly – those soldiers were. Many of them, after the four terrible years of slaughter during the 1914–18 war, had actually volunteered for the Black and Tans army. War coarsens and desensitises men. Killing became easy after their war experiences, and it was Ireland's misfortune that her people suffered so much indignity and loss.

Inevitably, my father in Athea, some thirty miles from Ahanagran where my mother lived (then unknown to him), was drawn into the struggle. Indeed, he took a very active part and achieved the rank of platoon commander. While continuing work on his father Tom Moran's farm, he attended meetings, drilled his men, hid people on the run, got some out to America and planned guerrilla action to hassle the occupying forces.

As the cards fell, he never killed anyone – and for this he was grateful in his old age. There was one tragic event in which he was closely involved, to such an extent that we had it related in song and in story throughout childhood. It was the story of the Boys of Knockanure, and it occurred at a high point of the Troubles. He was personally and closely acquainted with 'Walsh and Lyons' and 'the Dalton boy', who were summarily executed in the valley of Knockanure. My father's name was Con and, like him, the fourth member of that ill-fated group was also called Con. This young man, our cousin Con Dee, was the only one to escape alive.

The day the Black and Tans caught up with them, my father was saving the hay in a meadow, on the other side of the hill. Another farmer saw four young men enter the valley and, from his position higher up, he also saw a lorryload of soldiers coming up behind them. He signalled frantically, but they thought he was giving a friendly wave and the doomed youngsters waved back. He was too far away for his voice to reach and he watched the subsequent events in growing horror.

Those four lads were on the run and had prices on their heads, so one assumes they were active members of the Old IRA, in the way my father was. Feeling secure and confident on their home ground, they stopped at a bridge that spanned the sunlit river Feale and started to smoke. The bridge was close to a sharp bend and seconds later the lorry full of soldiers came round the corner. There was no time to run and no place to hide. In seconds they were surrounded and identified. Only one was over twenty.

A firing squad was quickly appointed and lined up to shoot them. As luck, or Divine Providence, would have it, Con Dee was placed fourth in the line-up. One by one the other unfortunate young men fell in sudden death. Before the 1916 Rising, during the first two years of the Great War, Con Dee had served in the British Army. At a time when everyone was poor, the army was a job – fairly well paid and offering unknown adventure. In the same unit as Con Dee there had been a young English soldier with whom he had become friends.

By an extraordinary intervention of Fate, this very man was a member of the firing party. Recognition was mutual as he raised his rifle and, with an infinitesimal jerk of the gun, he indicated to Con that he'd give him a chance. Con never needed more than half a chance. As the bullet whistled past his ear, he dived backwards and rolled down-hill. He had the presence of mind to light the furze as he went. The wind did the rest: in seconds a smokescreen hid him from view. Now, Con knew every inch of that ground. He had grown up there, wandered through it in the long holidays and fished in the river Feale. Although the surprised Tans jumped quickly over the low wall, they were too late. Con Dee not only escaped from them but, much later, managed to reach the coast and take ship for America. The Atlantic may have been a 'bowl of bitter tears', as President Kennedy once called it, for many immigrant Irish, but it was also the path to success and opportunity.

My father found the ending of Con Dee's story very sad. His own people, friends from around Athea and Ballylongford, found his escape inexplicable and many would not accept that it was due to a near miraculous coincidence. Dark whispers soon suggested that he was in league with the Tans and his escape had been manipulated. Nothing could have been further from the truth. Con Dee was as loyal to Ireland as Sarsfield or de Valera. Years later, when he returned to a free, greatly changed Ireland as a middle-aged man, he was met even then with a wall of sullen suspicion. Such lack of trust from his own folk resulted in bitter heartbreak and he never returned to Limerick again. (See Fergal Keane's version of this event in his book *Wounds*.)

My father heard the shots that killed the lads that day and imme-diately returned home. That evening, in the village of Athea, every young man of similar age was lined up, searched and questioned by power-drunk Tans. A very nervous young man stood beside my father in the line-up, one who had nothing whatever to do with politics. He was shaking in his shoes. Let's call him Bill Mulvaney.

'Don't, on any account, tell them your real name,' he hissed to my father, as they came down the line. Seconds later, a hard-faced Black and Tan stood in front of Bill and barked at him, 'Your name?'

'J-J-John O'Shea,' came the stuttered reply. They searched him roughly, noted down the name and turned to Daddy. 'Your name?'

'Bill Mulvaney,' he said firmly – hearing, with quickly suppressed amusement, the strangulated sound from Bill beside him. Later, Bill's private exchanges with my father are best imagined.

Dad was one of the volunteers who shouldered the coffins of the three murdered youngsters at their funeral, two days later. All those who carried the coffins were arrested and taken about fifteen miles away in lorries. Then they were let out and ordered to run, while bullets spat and ricocheted around them. The shots were to frighten rather than kill. Perhaps even the Tans had had enough of killing for that week.

In *Ballads from the Pubs of Ireland*, James N. Healy admits that the origin of the song about the lads shot in Knockanure was shrouded in mystery. A note in the preface ascribed it, with some qualifications, to Brian MacMahon, who altered it slightly. In fact, my father knew the author very well. He lived within walking distance of Athea in a place called Knocknaboul. He was called Jim Kiely and he was unable to read or write. He composed the song and my father wrote it down for him. Both of them are long dead now, but I'd like to set the record straight.

From 'The Valley of Knockanure' by Jim Kiely:

> You may speak and sing about Easter week,
> And the heroes of 'ninety-eight,
> Of the Fenian men who roamed the glens
> In victory or defeat.
> Their names on history's page are told,
> Their memory will endure,
> Not a song was sung for our darling sons
> In the valley of Knockanure.
>
> There was Walsh and Lyons and the Dalton boy
> They were young and in their pride,
> In every house, in every town
> They were always side by side.
> The Republic bold they did uphold,
> Though outlawed on the moor
> And side by side they fought and died
> In the valley of Knockanure.

'Twas on a neighbouring hillside
We listened with calm dismay,
In every house, in every town
A maiden knelt to pray.
They're closing in around them now
With rifle fire so sure
And Lyons is dead and Dalton's down
In the valley of Knockanure.

But ere the guns could seal their fate
Con Dee had broken through,
With a prayer to God, he spurned the sod
As against the hill he flew.
The bullets tore his flesh in two,
Yet he cried with passion pure,
'Revenge I'll get for my comrades' death
In the valley of Knockanure.'

Despite my parents' experience with the Black and Tans, they did not rear us to be anti-British. My father was a fair and honourable man, who never denied the moral integrity of the individual Englishman and always held that they made staunch friends. When two of his daughters subsequently married Englishmen, his concern was for their happiness and not for ancient feuds. He thought it right and proper that history should honour those who fell in places like Knockanure, but he reminded us too, that Britain lost twenty thousand men in one day at the Somme, proving nothing perhaps but the iniquity of war.

He was appalled when civil war broke out briefly in Ireland after the British withdrawal in the 1920s. He told us later that when Michael Collins was assassinated he decided that the fight for Irish freedom had degenerated into 'Pure blackguarding!' – a favourite phrase of his.

He promptly withdrew from all active participation and concentrated on his farming. Nevertheless, he not only received an official medal in 1946, but merited full military honours at his funeral in 1975.

9
Growing Up On a Farm

It was normal practice in the 1940s for farmer's wives to make their pin money through egg and chicken production. Naturally, all hens were free range and required the minimum of attention. They were fed twice a day and put themselves to bed each evening. Geese were even less trouble. They ate grass all round the house and came into the yard for a meal at sundown. Towards Christmas, they were sold or given as presents. One year, when our flock of geese was reduced to about six, my father got to know them quite well and he even gave them names.

A farmer who came from somewhere near Ballycotton – we never knew exactly where, but it was about eight miles away – arrived to buy the whole batch of them. He took them in a van and they squawked all the way down the avenue. We were a bit sad to see them go since we knew they were destined to be someone's dinner. We can only assume that the buyer, a Mr Burke, put them in a loose pen near his house. Certain it is that a little later on, when their feeding time came around, they rose majestically into the air, wheeled once or twice for direction and headed back to Brookedale.

After milking that evening, Daddy was astonished to see the same six geese waddling noisily into the yard. The long flight and the sea air had given them a keen appetite. The incident appealed to Dad's sardonic sense of humour. He decided there were immense possibilities in those geese. They could have become an excellent source of income, but his natural honesty prevented him from selling them again several times that year. I cannot remember their ultimate fate. Maybe the fox got one or two, for Brookedale was plagued with foxes and hawks, which preyed on livestock.

As I've mentioned, my mother usually kept a flock of turkeys. Each Christmas she raised forty or fifty and in their younger, more vulnerable state, they had to be protected from marauders. One hot day in August when I was about eleven, I was sent to the paddock to keep an eye on the turkeys. I had sneaked out the novel *Gone With the Wind*, which my father considered unsuitable for our green youth, and from a low sunny perch on a tree stump I glanced only occasionally at the grazing birds. A sudden kerfuffle and flapping of wings brought me instantly to my feet.

A long red fox about the size of a small collie, had his white teeth around the neck of the mother turkey. He was hauling her towards the glen while her offspring ran around in hysterical panic. Images of my mother's wrath lent wings to my feet and I charged at the fox yelling and waving my book about his foxy head.

Far from abandoning his prize, my antics seemed to give him an extra burst of energy. He growled through clenched teeth and glared at me from small glittering eyes. In seconds he had vanished, leaving a powerful smell behind, and of course myself, now dreading the encounter with my mother. She never forgot it, it seemed to me. She told the neighbours for miles around about her idiot daughter who had let the fox steal a turkey right from under her nose.

A short time later, when I was charged with the care of a flock of small chickens, I was much more careful. But, alas! My brother came out to have a word with me and in the minute we chatted, a hawk swept out of the sky and grabbed a young one. The struggling chick was almost too heavy for him and he had trouble getting airborne. Joseph and I ran shrieking behind him and, luckily, he dropped his prey, still alive and shivering. The next day we watched for the hawk and both of us followed him down the glen, walking blindly over furze and thorns, not daring to take our eyes off the graceful predator as it floated slowly above us on its way to its nest. Soon we pinpointed the tree it settled on and when the hawk flew off, Joseph elected to climb up. He was small, wiry and still in short trousers but he persevered, while I watched for the hawk from the ground, fearing she might return and claw out his eyes. When Joe reached the nest, he put its contents in his pockets and scrambled back. His excursion proved my mother was right to fear predators. The hawk had been helping herself from every local farm – Mellericks and Cahills, as well as our own. When we emptied Joseph's pockets on the ground, we found twenty-seven chicken legs, seven small rabbits' paws and one rather large yellow claw.

Our feathered flock could be diminished in many unexpected ways. When we were small, pre-school age, my mother always sent us for an afternoon sleep. She often tied mother hens by the leg on a loose rein in a shady place near the house to keep them close by. Beside one such hen, on a warm summer afternoon, lay my two-year-old sister Mary, sound asleep. When she woke up, she saw all the fluffy chicks skipping round their mother. In delight, the child clearly thought she had some new, active toys. She crept towards them, and when my mother came out, she was appalled to see her daughter catching the tiny chicks by their heads and chuckling as she whirled them round and round before throwing them over her shoulder. There were nine dead chickens on the ground behind her.

One night, soon after my experience with the fox that grabbed the mother turkey, we heard the hens creating a frantic din. My father reached the hen house first and found a dead fox, surrounded by furious young cockerels that had scratched and pecked at him in noisy fright. Dad dragged him out by the tail and went off to tell my mother of his amazing find. The moment he turned his back, the artful fox leaped to his feet and was off down the glen, like a bedraggled bullet. On that occasion he had killed very few hens, but the following Christmas he and his mate attacked the whole flock of turkeys in broad daylight and killed twenty-eight of them. We ate turkey until we were tired of it, and all of the neighbours received unexpected early presents.

The day after the turkey slaughter, the men formed a posse, took the dogs and a ferret and dug out the foxes' burrow. There was a second litter in it and they killed the little ones and hung them on trees near the house as a warning to other foxes that they had gone too far.

My brother Joseph longed to go on a proper fox hunt, with hounds and horses and the great camaraderie. Every St Stephen's Day, enthusiasts gathered in Dungourney and rode with the hounds through the countryside. In a farming community, where the fox did so much dam-age, this custom met with total approval. From the time Joseph could sit on a horse, he wanted to join the hunt, but my parents relented only when he was nine. Even then, he wasn't given the sprightly young Blackbird. Instead, my father entrusted him to Paddy, seven years old and sensibly staid for a child.

However, no one had taken the infectious excitement into consid-eration. Dozens of barking hounds, restless high-spirited horses – some of them promoted from the plough – and scores of enthusiastic, experienced riders all combined to create a heady atmosphere. Joseph barely had his feet in the shortened stirrups when our sober and stout Paddy sniffed the air, laid back his ears and took off at a lumbering gallop after the streaming dogs and yodelling riders. Paddy had never jumped a fence in his life, but he rose bravely with the others. He got his front legs over, shot Joseph ahead of him into a pond of dirty water and belly-flopped on the broad fence. With scarcely a glance, the others streamed past and when Joseph had extricated himself, Paddy, too, was free and going flat out after the rest. Young Joseph, wet and miserable, walked the five miles home and arrived to find a sedate Paddy, brushed and combed and peacefully eating his oats, none the worse for his adventure.

Joseph went on to become an expert jockey before he grew too tall, but I doubt if any heart-stopping race later on had quite the same enchantment as that first hunt out of Dungourney.

10

Alcohol

Unlike some families who saw their way of life diminished or destroyed by excessive alcohol, we were lucky that my father had little taste for it. He was a social drinker and indulged happily, but in moderation, when visitors came his way. Besides, alcohol was a luxury and he had no money to waste.

His brother, Frank, whom he greatly loved, was a man with a larger-than-life personality. He was wealthy and successful but his extraordinary friendship with Con, my father, survived the making of his vast fortune and the inevitable separation of business and distance. Each year, the two of them went on holiday together. My father entrusted the running of the farm to my mother and off he went for a few weeks with Frank.

Two or three times a year, Uncle Frank drove up in style. He was about six foot two and at least eighteen stone. Wherever he was, he became the instant focus of attention. Within five minutes of entering a pub, he'd decided what everyone was to drink, whose turn it was to buy the next round and, more surprisingly, what time the establishment was to close!

We seldom kept alcohol in the house, so Frank always arrived with a bottle of whiskey. Once, as he walked across the stone-flagged kitchen floor to hand it to my father, it slipped out of their hands and smashed to smithereens. The moment was like a wake. The two men gazed in horror at the widening circle of precious whiskey while visions of a cheerful, reminiscing evening went out of the unlubricated window. Sam licked it up a bit tentatively and clearly it grew on him as he delicately avoided fine slivers of glass and enthusiastically finished it.

For the only time in his life, our faithful Sam could not be persuaded to go for the cows that evening. Blind drunk, he gyrated round the yard, all dignity forgotten as he rolled on his back, legs in the air and snorted, like a pony, before he fell into a profound sleep. For months afterwards, the chink of glass was enough to bring him bounding hopefully to the door.

Uncle Frank loved to drink and, luckily, he had the kind of metabolism that caused his good humour to increase with every glass. His wife, Aunty Lizzie, a tiny, refined headmistress, was a lady of great piety. He relied on her virtue for his own salvation and he'd worked out a rather curious philosophy. 'I'm certain to go to Heaven,' he'd announce, if challenged. 'See the good wife I have! It's obvious she'll be high among the angels and therefore so will I. The Man Above would never break His own laws. What God has joined together, let no man put asunder! We were joined in matrimony and she'll pull me into Heaven after her. He'd never separate us.'

Though his wife disliked alcohol herself, she was companion and friend to her husband on as many social outings as possible. As she was so devout, she made a point of visiting any places of pilgrimage she could. Once, when our two families were on the way back from Lisdoonvarna, she asked the driver to stop at a holy well where the waters were said to have curative properties. While she said a short prayer, and we bottled some of the water, my father and Uncle Frank crept off to a nearby pub. Half an hour later, when they emerged, Frank had a speculative gleam in his eye. 'I'm told,' he announced to us all, 'that we're lucky to be travelling this road because it is famous for the number of its holy wells.' We were driving from Clare through Kerry to Cork, and for the next sixty miles, we discovered no fewer than seven holy wells, all miraculously situated next door to pubs. In the end, Aunty Lizzie outlived Uncle Frank by eight years – so we're not sure where he spent the waiting time!

Another drinking buddy of my father's was one Maurice Burke, who complained frequently about a sore throat. Eventually, he was persuaded to visit our local doctor. 'Doctor,' he stated firmly, 'you must help me – there's something wrong with my throat.'

The conscientious doctor examined him carefully but could not find either redness or swelling.

'Well, Maurice,' he explained, 'your throat is fine. There's no infection. What are your symptoms again?'

'Look, Doctor,' replied Maurice, 'there must be something wrong with that throat because two farms, a tractor and a shop have gone down it!'

Harvest threshing days in the 1940s were unforgettable experiences. Abler pens than mine have described them fully and my own memories endorse their comments. They were one of the major events of the year. My father, who loved people, was in his element. About twenty local men came to help. It was just accepted then that farmers helped each other in this way. For about three weeks every summer, Jack or Jim or Ned from our house would be off taking a turn at the neighbours' big day. Modern combine harvesters have cancelled out these social occasions, since two men can now do what it once took twenty to accomplish.

Back then, while my mother and several friends prepared the plain but abundant food, my father bought an enormous barrel of Guinness. Maybe time is deceptive but I never remember a cold or misty threshing day. The sun was always blazing down on a dozen men piking golden sheaves into the maw of the threshing machine while others, laughing and talking, tied the bags and trundled them away.

After school on those days, we children had our own allotted tasks. One was to carry gallons of frothy Guinness around to the ricks and pass them glass by glass to the hot, dusty men. That evening, we had a party. All the men stayed and often their wives came too. Proficiency with a flute, piano accordion or fiddle was taken for granted. Not one of the musicians had much in the way of formal teaching, but they produced a harmony of sound that lingers with me yet. Everyone sang or recited a poem and was cheered to the echo as the Guinness flowed freely. 'The Green Eye of the Little Yellow God' was my favourite poem until I heard Jim Sullivan recite 'Sam Magee'.

Our local Justice of the Peace, John-Joe Aherne, always sang 'Genevieve' – slightly off key, but welcome all the same. I remember being intrigued by the sight of a large lady, about thirteen stone, singing in a plaintive, rather sweet voice,

'Why stand I here, like a ghost and a shadow,
It's time I was moving, time I passed on.'

'A ghost and a shadow!' whispered Joseph, standing behind me. 'Some ghost!'

I giggled then but now, of course, they are all gone to join the shades of their ancestors, even Joseph himself, whose years were cut short: he died of cardiac arrest, aged just forty-two.

Perhaps because of the alien origin of many Irish laws down through the years – since Henry Plantagenet in the twelfth century established his suzerainty over Strongbow and the local chieftains of the south, the Irish have resisted the imposition of regulations. To circumvent them became a source of pride. Not only were laws regarded as a restriction of personal freedom, but it was considered they assumed an unwarranted right to intervene in people's private lives – in a way that unjustly parted them from their money. After the Easter Rising of 1916 and the subsequent establishment of the Republic, the Irish government came up against this age-old, ingrained resentment of regimentation.

When I was a child and for many years later, the illegal brewing of poteen, a very strong alcohol made from potatoes or barley, was a serious offence. Six months in jail or a heavy fine was the common penalty. This did not stop it being made, but a brotherhood of silence developed. The quality of the poteen varied considerably, of course. It could be 100 per cent proof, strong enough to take the roof off your mouth or be used as cigarette-lighter fuel if you were inclined to waste it. My brother – at seventeen – was courting the pretty daughter of Dick Barry, the landlord at Barry's pub. Now, Dick always kept his choice supply of poteen for favoured customers. Poteen is the colour of clear water and could be slipped into orange or tonic water, under the very nose of the law – though not too closely under it, for it has a pungent smell.

Once, after Joe had collected a dozen bottles from a hillside still outside Cork, he observed a vigilant police car sitting on his tail. He drove along sedately, carefully observing the rules of the road. To his disappointment, the sirens went off after a few miles, and he was signalled to pull over. Mystified and swearing under his breath, he stopped, got out and courteously inquired if he could help the officer.

'Your rear light is gone, sir,' pointed out the policeman. With a sigh of relief, Joseph apologised and said it was a bit erratic but a good wallop soon restored it. Suiting the action to the word, he thumped the boot. To his dismay, it shot open, revealing the bottles of poteen to the sky. Hastily he shut it down and he was lucky that the policeman was studying the lights and never noticed his panic, especially as the light came on instantly and all was well.

Uncle Frank, who respected only God's law and those he had made himself, naturally had his own illicit still. At the time, he was still creamery manager of Mountcollins, and well out of sight, away at the back, many gallons of poteen were secretly brewed. Unfortunately, a young and zealous government inspector arrived without notice and stumbled across it. The man was walking unaccompanied about the creamery premises and spotted the tell-tale smoke, as well as the several men entering and leaving the area of the still. Having confirmed its existence, he stormed into Uncle Frank's office. It never entered his law-abiding head that Frank himself had set it up.

'I have bad news for you, Mr Moran,' he began. 'You won't credit this, but four of your own men are brewing poteen, right *here* on the premises!'

He was unprepared for the fury he provoked. My uncle, a consummate actor, leaped to his enormous feet, positively bellowing with rage. 'Never!' he thundered. 'I'll soon deal with that. Leave it to me, sir. I'll send for the bastards this minute and I'll sack the lot! No, no! *Don't* appeal to me!' he continued to the astonished inspector, who hadn't even dreamed of appealing to him.

Uncle Frank was still roaring. 'These fellows have families, sir! It will be hard for them to get other jobs, but they have brought that on themselves! I'll put the word out myself and I'll have that still dismantled and burned within the hour.'

The men were summoned and lined up. The sheer speed of events mesmerised the inexperienced inspector. He was clearly impressed at the sight of the owner bellowing righteous indignation at men in clear awe of him. Seeing that justice was being done, the inspector was soon bowing his thanks and approval. The four delinquents, almost tripping over their hangdog expressions, were given their cards. Loudly, and with bitter recriminations, Uncle Frank ordered them all off the premises. They slunk away, looking cowed and utterly miserable. The satisfied inspector soon followed them.

An hour later, the men were back, grinning like conspirators. Glasses of poteen were passed around and Frank got down to the business of future security. He was never caught again. Once, after his retirement, during a visit home, I asked him in a city pub if he still had his connections in the poteen world.

'Where could I get some poteen?' I inquired, in a perfectly normal, audible voice.

Instantly he went into a routine of affronted respectability. 'Listen, girleen,' he said loudly. 'Drinking poteen is against the law. Nobody around here would have anything to do with that kind of thing.'

Feeling a bit abashed, I said no more but fairly late that night, a woman came to our door and whispered that she had a little gift for Frank's niece. She passed in a 7-Up lemonade bottle, which proved to contain poteen. Next day, as I said goodbye, he asked me if I knew the lady.

'No,' I replied.

'Well, keep it to yourself,' he said, 'but she's the wife of the chief superintendent of the police for — City. He owes me a few favours.'

11

Social Life

There were three established social centres in the lives of our farming community. Every Sunday, hail, rain or snow, we would gather for Mass in Mogeely. Where today people run an appraising eye over each other's cars, we viewed one another for the best turned-out pony and trap. Our neighbours, the Cahills, always had the smartest equipage and their spirited horses swept them down the two miles to Mogeely in a bare ten minutes. If the cry 'The Cahills are gone!' went up, we knew we were late unless his Reverence was delayed, and that was rare.

In those days of low wages, everyone contributed a penny to the collection. This was a reasonable percentage of their pay but, even so, the priest was on very limited funds. A workman called Pats Griffin, not at all well off, once fumbled awkwardly in his pocket as the collection plate came round. By mistake he gave half a crown (about the size of a penny, but worth two shillings and sixpence). He nearly fainted as he saw the plate vanish with his silver coin gleaming amongst the coppers. After Mass, news of the catastrophe spread quickly from man to man. His friends gathered round him in silent helpless sympathy. Pats was so miserable that, in the end, one brave man urged him to go round to the Sacristy and ask for his money back.

'Just tell the priest what happened,' the man said. 'He'll understand.'

The parish priest had been overjoyed to spot the munificent half-crown among the pennies. He had just inquired as to the source of this generous windfall when Pats appeared hesitantly in the doorway. Before he could open his mouth, the priest greeted him with praise and enthusiasm. 'Pats!' he said, 'My dear man, come in, come in, come in – I tell you, God will reward your generosity this day. What a sacrifice you made! I know – don't think I don't – that you have to watch your money. To give so unselfishly will bring a rich reward in Heaven. The angels note our every act. Pats, you are a fine example to the whole parish.'

Overwhelmed by all this effusive gratitude, Pats didn't have the heart to tell him the purpose of his visit. He murmured some deprecatory noises and walked out. He returned to his friends in a furious temper.

'Did you get it?' they choroused.

'No, I did not,' he replied savagely. 'I've given it to God . . . and He can go to Hell with it!'

The other great centre for social get-togethers was known as the Stage. This was a wooden platform set up beside a convenient roadside space, and there people of every age gathered to dance the Set: the four-hand reel, the 'Siege of Ennis' and the 'Walls of Limerick'. There was no drink available (the nearest pub was two miles away) and the dancers had to be content with the music, the company and the peace of an Irish summer night. Usually, the fiddle and the piano-accordion were the instruments used. We heard that the parish priest was not in favour of those weekly dances. He thundered about them occasionally from the pulpit as 'occasions of sin'. He was greatly respected but he thundered about a lot of things. Once he spoke so graphically and enthusiastically about Hell that one old lady was heard to murmur to her neighbour, 'Father M. knows so much about Hell, you'd think he'd just come back from a fortnight's holiday there.'

One evening, as it grew dark, Father M. visited the Stage gathering for himself, to confirm his disapproval. His alert parishioners saw him coming and melted tactfully away. In the half-darkness, the fiddler, who was blind anyway, continued his playing, unaware of the looming figure of the parish priest.

'Mike,' Father M. said crossly, into his ear. 'Do you know you're doing the work of the devil?'

Inevitably, Mike replied, in an expressionless voice, 'No, but whistle it for me and I'll have a go.'

It happened that the Stage was burned down later that year and I suppose there were some who wondered if fire and brimstone had descended on it.

The other great chance to socialise – apart from harvest threshings – came when someone died. A wake was both a touching and lengthy affair. The dear departed was instantly canonised by all and sundry. He or she was laid out, suitably robed, in a largish room surrounded by thick, blessed and lighted candles, as well as many flowers.

The first one I saw was Mrs Terry's. She was a very old lady who had lived with her son in a little cottage less than half a mile away. Her only daughter, Annie, had gone to America. The four of us had called in to see Mrs Terry every evening after school, for drinks of water and the odd sweet. If we chanced to meet her horse, Maggie, on the way, we all climbed onto her wide back and rode her gently home.

We never saw Mrs Terry without hearing a grieving reference to Annie. Not once in ten years did she write to her mother, but Mrs Terry never gave up hope. Annie's picture was prominently displayed beside a picture of the Sacred Heart, but whether she was alive or dead no one ever knew. One of my first fits of helpless anger was directed against the unknown Annie, whose coldness had grieved our beloved Mrs Terry so much. Her son, Bill, provided the welcome at her wake. All day and half the night people came in, shook his hand, murmured, 'I'm sorry for your trouble,' and stayed to pray awhile and eat ham sandwiches with their whiskey or sherry.

The Irish can be incredibly kind people. They often go to great lengths to find something, anything positive to say about the deceased. If he was an absolute old skinflint who'd never had a good word for anyone, they'd sheer away from his personality to his actions. Of one such, I heard a man say, 'Didn't he grow gorgeous flowers?' or 'That man's hens were the best layers around these parts.'

Usually, though, virtue was easy enough to distinguish and the comments were warm and genuine. Someone said of my father, 'This is a funny old world. We're going to miss him. He was everyone's friend.'

A Seven-Year-Old Walks With Her Father

I remember . . .
Your powerful shoulders strong against the sky
Almost blotting out the stars,
The infinite twinkling darkness

Lifting like wine above us –
While your own tobaccoed incense
Sent a sweetness through the night
Chasing quiet birds.

Curious and confident, I queried their destination,
Though drifting dangers hid beneath the trees,
And nightingales sang in soft elation
While cowslips slept in hollows of the breeze.
'Their mothers are waiting to put them to bed,
Now hold my hand and be good,' you said.

I held it tight in trusting faith,
For you were always on my side
Protecting your small Kate.

You were my bulwark, Dad, 'gainst every wrong,
So full of kindliness and joyous song
That well I knew your hard and calloused hands
Would catch the arrows Fortune sent along.

The thought that there would come a time
When you would cease to be
Was farther then than were the stars from me.

So – I remember you now, Dad, with smiles and tears.
Though you've been gone, these fifty years.

With a handshake or a hug, the bereaved were assured of a meeting in Eternity. Death was no more than a stop on a journey, after all. One day, the family of God would be together in their Father's house, where all wrongs would be righted and all separations at an end. Those country wakes, which are still observed today, had a profoundly comforting effect. By the time the grieving relatives had shaken hundreds of hands, cut thousands of sandwiches and poured out scores of drinks, their shocked minds began to accept the stark fact of death and the therapeutic process of healing could begin.

It was true, however, that every detail of the final illness would be mulled over and blame liberally applied if help hadn't arrived in time.

Usually, any relatives who happened to be priests were invited to grace the Requiem Mass. My mother heard a curious old lady, whose hearing was not too sound, reporting her triumphant discovery when one dead man's daughter mentioned to a friend, 'Father Brendan will of course officiate.'

'Do you know what killed him in the end?' whispered the old lady, a few minutes later. 'It was a fish he ate . . .'

I never saw the kindly people who attended as curiosity-seekers. Their mere presence was accepted for what it was – a sign of respect for the dead, and a helping hand for the living.

12

A House for Two Pounds

Our home in Brookedale was really quite peculiar in its physical characteristics. The house itself had been the staff quarters of the enormous Brookedale House, which once belonged to Lord Brookeborough and was burned down during some political upheaval. Our part of it survived the fire and was said to be 'crawling with ghosts'. It was a three-storey building and the whole of the ground floor was a windowless cellar, with the entrance blocked up – at least, until my brother and I found our way in. Our living space began in the first storey and this was reached by fourteen concrete steps from the yard at one end and a rigid little bridge across a ten-foot-wide dry moat on the other. Had the need arisen, we could have withstood a siege. The second storey consisted of large, spacious, pine-lined rooms, which we didn't really require and seldom used, into which hurtling bats came at eventide, silently flying down dark corridors and swerving out of our way with the propulsion of their own radar.

When we took up residence, the floor immediately above the kitchen needed stronger joists, but before my father could replace them, his friend Jack Mackessey walked heavily across one morning and fell straight through. At the time, we were seated round the breakfast table when his enormous wellington boot came through the ceiling, followed quickly by a roar, his large body and a shower of plaster. A cascade of debris landed on the table and smashed all the china.

'Try the stairs, Jack. They're not quicker, but they're safer,' said my father, good-humouredly, as Jack shook the plaster from his red-gold hair and the eggshells off his knees.

There was no central heating in Brookedale and all the rooms were warmed by open wood fires. Missing the peat, so plentiful around Limerick, Dad sent home for a couple of tons of it when we first arrived. Carting it from Mogeely station over a few miles of winding country roads proved to be so arduous that he never did it again.

It was rare for us to have toys of any kind when we were children, but we did have lots of cuddly young animals. Sometimes, when the early corn was cut, nests of rabbits and young corncrakes would be uncovered. So, as well as puppies, kittens and lambs, we often had pet rabbits and fledgling birds to rear. Once, when I was about eight, I met the men returning from the fields and my father produced from his pocket a perfect baby rabbit with, unusually, a shiny black coat. The little wild creature leaped and struggled as he was handed over, but I held on to him firmly. That evening I refused to let him out of my sight and I even sneaked him into bed. I remember seeing his outline in the firelight as he sat on my pillow, twitching his whiskers before I fell asleep.

Several hours later, I awakened to an almighty commotion. In the semi-darkness, an enormous figure was leaping and crashing over furniture, walloping distant corners of the room while yelling for my mother. Dad had been out when we'd gone to bed. As was his custom, he went round to each of us, sprinkling holy water on those asleep and saying goodnight to those still awake. Imagine his fear, when he saw what he took to be a large rat running across our bedroom floor. He grabbed a rush-mat inside the door, rolled it into a weapon and lashed out ferociously. The firelight elongated his leaping shadow and made me think, at first, that a wild creature had broken into my sleep.

'Nora, there's a rat in here!' he shouted to my mother, as he dived under the second bed. I saw my little rabbit break free and run for the chimney.

'It's my rabbit!' I screamed. 'Leave him alone, Dad!'

Relieved and realising his mistake, he abandoned the chase and tiptoed out – as if anyone was still sleeping then! I got up in tears and searched the room in vain, for my pet. Two days later, Birdie found his little dead body amongst the ashes. Either in fear or through instinct, he'd gone for the warmth and had been smothered by the cooling ash.

We had one novel item in our household – an indoor toilet. I doubt if any other farmhouse in County Cork boasted such a luxury in those days. However, with all the empty rooms, Brookedale was always terribly cold and draughty. In 1950, my father decided to build a new house. This was a particularly courageous project, since his main assets, apart from the farm, were his heart, his strength – and the abundant raw materials around Brookedale. Plans were made, and the night before the builders were due, he stood in the old kitchen, thoughtfully jingling the coins in his pocket.

'How much is in there, Dad?' inquired Mary.

'Two pounds,' he replied. 'And you won't meet many men in your lifetime who are ready to start building their new house with only two pounds in their pocket.'

How right he was!

His brother Frank organised an initial loan for him, from the Brosna Provider fund, which Frank controlled as creamery manager. Apart from that sum, every stone, slate, floorboard and wooden window-frame came from Brookedale. There was even a sand quarry to help make the cement and plaster. Some of the ancient foundation stones of the old Brookedale House were used. The neighbours came in to offer advice. When they saw the layout of the site, they threw their hands up in dismay.

'Don't you know the old Protestant chapel of the Brookeboroughs used to stand right here? It's full of ghosts and banshees. Could you ever have peace there?' Dad, who had his own strong faith and was not superstitious, ignored the Jeremiahs and went ahead. Besides, he said, any ancient place of Christian worship was surely holy ground, and if it wasn't, we could soon make it so.

The neighbours came again when the building was half up and sighed dolefully at the position of the fireplace in the new kitchen.

'That's the very spot where the Protestant altar used to be – and where English landlords prayed for strength to subdue the Irish.'

Again, my father took no notice, but oddly enough, when the first cosy fire was lit in the huge kitchen, the chimney refused to draw – no doubt the builder was at fault. Black, billowy smoke filled the room and guests went into the yard with streaming eyes and choking coughs.

'What did I tell you?' they kept asking one another. 'The souls of the persecuted are thick around here.'

No matter how the flues were altered, a special stove had to be installed eventually. After that, a large swarm of bees settled in the chimney and burrowed into the very fabric. Their honey, soaking through the walls, became a serious nuisance in the master bedroom upstairs. A similar hive took up residence in the old house and the honey was harvested by Mary and our cousin Francis.

After the repairs and regular Masses in the home, when we took our turn for 'the Stations' (Mass in the house), the place settled down and my parents were proud of its convenience and comfort. Electricity was installed in 1953 and inevitably, in due course, came television. This invention confused and bewildered some of the old-timers. My father was once watching a re-enactment of a local skirmish from the time of the Black and Tans, when his elderly visitor shook his head in disbelief.

'Don't believe a word of that, Boss,' he said to Dad. 'I was there. I tell you, and I can assure you there wasn't a camera next or nigh the place.'

Superseded by the newer, smarter edifice, the old house was left to crumble into ruin, surrounded by encroaching trees.

> A house that has sheltered a baby's laugh,
> And held up his stumbling feet,
> Is the saddest sight when it's left alone
> That ever the eye could meet.

Alfred Joyce Kilmer

13
Rich Personalities and a Bit of Danger

I suppose there are some who feel that our lives are made up of trifles, and maybe they are right, but as Michelangelo is reputed to have said: 'Trifles are only trifles, but trifles make perfection – and perfection is no trifle.'

In retrospect, I remember with appreciation the courage of the people I knew. Maria B. sliced off her finger while chopping wood one day. She sought it among the chippings and sawdust and popped it into her apron pocket. With a towel wrapped around her hand, she ran the half-mile to the doctor. In appalled silence, he studied the mutilated hand and sighed. 'I'll have to cauterise that, Maria,' he said. 'It will hurt, but it will stop the infection.'

'What about my finger?' inquired Maria.

'I'm afraid you'll have to get used to being without it,' he replied.

Maria got up and walked over to the tap in the corner. With her other hand, she fumbled in her pocket for the missing finger. With difficulty, she turned on the water and gave the finger a quick rinse. 'Doctor,' she said, turning around. 'Do me a favour – I'm a busy mother with six children and I need all my fingers. Sew it on, please.' There was neither ice nor micro-surgery nor anaesthetic available, only the thirty years' experience of a good country doctor and time running out.

Without more delay he neatly stitched back the finger, put it in bandaged splints and sent her home. She was lucky, very lucky. When the bandages came off the finger was stiff but sound, and within a year it was usable. Thirty years later, my three-year-old nephew had a similar accident but lost all four fingers of his right hand, because our local doctor, trusting to the dramatic advances of modern medicine and distrusting himself, waited for a prestigious micro-surgeon who took six hours to come from Limerick – while the fingers died.

On our farm our incoming money matched our outgoing commitments so we were never bothered by tax demands. I heard Dad mutter that they 'attacked' him once a year, without much satisfaction, I'm sure. However, in the early 1950s, a new awareness crept into Ireland. All kinds of facts had to be documented and the hours of farm labourers had to be reckoned for overtime. Constant inspectors turned up to ask searching questions. Once, when Dad was under a tractor in his usual working clothes, a new apparition appeared from the tax office.

'My good man,' he said, to my rumpled, scruffy-looking father. 'Go in and tell your master that Mr O'Brien from the tax office is here to see him.' Dad opened his mouth to introduce himself, but the man said brusquely, 'Now be quick about it, I'm in a hurry . . .' My father went in, shaved, brushed his hair and changed. He then appeared out of the other door. He swore the man never recognised him, for he came forward, oozing charm and smiling like a shark. He wanted to know the full details about wages and hours for the men on the farm, the boy in the yard and the maid in the house.

'Thank you, thank you, Mr Moran,' said the visitor. 'And will that be all? Have you anyone else working here?'

'Well,' responded my father, 'I have a poor old fellow for general duties.'

'What are his hours?' asked the man, sharply, getting out his notebook again.

'He works from first light until darkness falls. Sometimes he'll get up at night to see to the pregnant animals.'

'And what do you pay him?' inquired the now-interested taxman.

'Actually, he's easy to pay,' said Dad. 'I give him a few shillings every week for a drink and tobacco and a suit of clothes every two years or so – and his meals, of course.'

'Well, Mr Moran, I have to tell you that I must interview this man. I have to insist. Will you get him, please?'

'No need for that,' answered Dad. 'You're talking to him.'

*

The Dungourney river flowed lazily past our land and offered us, as children, unlimited opportunities for adventure. I suppose the Emerald Isle gets its name from its green fields and seemingly endless rain. Despite 'the soft summer gladness of the rain', we rarely saw the river in flood. Yet one wet day in high summer, I looked out of the windows of our hilltop farmhouse and saw the valley filled with a brown, swirling mass of moving water. We were safe, but the house immediately below us, on the stretch called the Inch, was only half visible, for the waters were already past the lower-storey windows. I was almost fourteen and I'd never seen such a mighty flood before. In places, it was ten feet deep because a whole stretch of riverbank had broken away.

Unfortunately, my father was visiting his brother Frank, and Jim Sullivan had a broken leg, deep in plaster. I was at home only because it was holiday time and, at fourteen, happy to be escaping school. The minor disaster was exacerbated by the very recent arrival of the house's new occupants. The Howes, Mamie and Michael, had come from America only two days before to take up residence. Like a lot of Irish-Americans, they were full of romantic notions about the land of their fathers and they were looking forward to a warm, friendly community where their welcome was secure and their five children safe. Now, on the third morning, they woke up to a roaring, wet world, which seemed to rock their ancient house to its foundations.

I had been reading a lot of *Girls' Crystal* books lately in which a young woman called Sylvia performed near miracles of ingenuity and leadership. Watching the waves rippling in and out of the Howes' ground-floor windows, I decided this was my chance for fame and maybe medals. I dreamed on a little. I saw myself being interviewed and modestly disclaiming all heroism while the grateful Howe family wept with emotion and poured wine into my shoes.

The hay-float was still in the yard and good, faithful Paddy was grazing above the water line. First, I caught and tackled him, then, under Jim's approving direction, I backed him between the shafts of the float. Next I added a small ladder and some rope and directed Paddy towards the road entrance, which was still dry. As we went down the hill, all went well until we were deeply into the water. Placid Paddy swam, though the occasional bush below the surface got up his nose sometimes and he veered off course for a while. The water was lapping over his back when we reached the house and hailed the unfortunate family.

They were all upstairs, damp and stranded, the baby yelling non-stop. The large hay-float did exactly that. It floated beautifully but it was rather wobbly. I had to keep the horse swimming in roughly the same spot while I propped up the ladder. Leaning against the foot of it and heaving on the reins, I shouted at them to come down.

Mr Howe sized up the situation quickly. He managed to climb out in giant waders which reached his hips, using all his strength to hold the ladder steady while his eldest son brought down the baby strapped to his back. One by one the rest descended, and their black-haired mother came last. They had not even finished their unpacking and I could see their trunks bobbing and knocking into each other in the hallway. Mamie, I discovered later, had some exquisite dresses that could only be dry-cleaned. They were damaged beyond repair by the muddy water.

As the laden hay-float pulled away, I heard three-year-old Maureen give a shriek of protest as her sopping yellow teddy bear floated into our wake. Faithful, stolid Paddy turned his head towards Brookedale, and a few minutes later, my mother welcomed the whole shivering family with hot soup and blankets. Even the crying baby drifted into sleepy silence before the fire. I was kept so busy attending to them that my moment of glory passed unnoticed even by myself.

On his return, my father commented, 'Well done, Kate!' and with that I had to be content. However, Mrs Howe became my close and admired friend, though I nearly lost my life a few months later while doing her a good turn.

Mrs Howe asked me to babysit while she and her husband went to a ceilidh – an evening of music and dancing. She was blessed with a family of healthy good looks, but one of the boys was a young Adonis. He had rich, luxuriant brown-gold hair and deep blue eyes. He walked with a natural grace. Conscious perhaps of potential male beauty above the average, he was spoiled and over-confident, even as a child of eleven. He had none of the shrinking, delightful shyness of his brother or sisters. He spoke with a Brooklyn twang and we lined up just to listen to him. He was far more advanced at eleven than we were at fourteen. We found it extraordinarily daring that he was openly prepared to flout authority. When he discovered he could be caned at Ballintotas School, he said flatly that if anyone laid a finger on him, he would leave school for good, and we knew he meant it. His parents loved him and were proud of him, but they were a bit unsure how to manage his precocious personality. They knew he couldn't tolerate much frustration and were reluctant to test him.

The evening I went down to sit with the baby and toddler, his mother asked me to keep him out of their bedroom because the children were already asleep. I sat in there with the little ones, leaving the others to their own devices. About an hour later, the door slammed open. Their puppy and a scared black cat shot into the room. On their heels came Edgar, as I shall call him, brandishing a broom and laughing loudly. He was roughly the age of my brother, and when the chips were down, I reckoned I could get the better of him. I ordered him out without ceremony and without the terrified animals. When he refused, I pushed him out and slammed the door, putting a chair against it. Unused to and indeed unaware of the differences between American culture and our own law-abiding family, I was quite unworried as I settled my young charges once more. I was in the middle of a quiet rendering of 'The Kerry Dances', when Edgar crashed through the door armed with his father's loaded rifle. Eleven he might have been, but he was white with rage as he ordered me to release the cat and dog. I can only remember a blinding fury of my own as I jumped up.

'Mind your sisters!' I yelled. As his glance flicked over the golden heads on the cushion, I threw myself across the barrel of the gun so that it pointed out under my arm. I wrenched him round in a circle so that the bullet would go through the window. Taken by surprise, he wrestled desperately, but I was bigger and a bit more aware of the danger. I took the gun from him before he could fire it. He ran outside then and hid, while I sat triumphantly with the gun across my knees.

After a while, though, I began to worry that young Edgar might be seeking out a second gun. I slipped quietly out of the back door and rushed home to tell my father.

A neighbour was visiting and they all listened, aghast, to my story. Every adult in the house came down with me, and when the Howes returned, they were greeted by five indignant babysitters. Dad had some taut words with Mr Howe about the dangers of leaving loaded guns within reach of children. Edgar, it was decided, had seen too many Westerns and was, of course, too young to appreciate the tragedy that might have ensued. We became friends during the next year, partly because he learned to ride on one of our farm horses and partly because I loved being seen in the company of such a handsome boy with the gorgeous accent.

I suppose this unique event in my childhood foreshadowed modern America's preoccupation with guns and the dreadful deeds that have blighted so many families. We knew there was a farm shotgun in our house but it was never within our reach, and not in our wildest childhood dreams would we have dared to touch it.

14
Neighbours

My parents had two very close friends – Mai and Jerry Corbett. Their farm was a few miles away by road, but as the crow flies, about half an hour across the glen. They were from Kerry and that fact alone ensured their initial welcome.

Jerry was witty, well-read and absolutely dependable: 'a man as honest, as simple, as natural as you would meet in a day's walking' in Padraig Pearse's words. Mai was nervous and spiritual, my mother's trusted confidante in everything. As I recall her, she was past the first bloom of youth, but still retained some of her earlier loveliness. When Jerry had fallen in love with her, she'd been just seventeen and her alarmed parents forbade all contact between them. To make doubly certain, they took the precaution of sending her to an aunt in America in the hope that distance would surely lessen the enchantment of Jerry's handsome face. Their plans miscarried. The resourceful Jerry made his way to Cobh and from there worked his passage to America in order to find Mai. Three months later, they were married and both families had to accept the *fait accompli*.

Greatly to their disappointment, they had no children and in many ways they became surrogate parents to the four of us. Jerry played the bagpipes and their wild, skirling notes or anguished keening whirled across the valley on many a long summer evening. Jerry knew he needed no invitation to visit our house and he and Mai often made the trip across the glen. My long-suffering mother drew the line at bagpipes in the house, so Jerry played as he walked up and down the yard while my father beamed appreciatively from an upturned milk-churn, or even accompanied him on the flute. We children leaned across the half-door and drank it all in.

Jerry and my father were not merely musical friends, they were progressive and innovative farmers and shared all the latest technological improvements in the 'agri-business'. For instance, soon after the war, when new, improved agricultural machinery appeared on the market, my father and Jerry clubbed together to buy a Massey-Harris reaper-and-binder. It cost all of two hundred pounds, a vast sum in those days. I still recall the pride with which the two men displayed this shining wonder in our farmyard.

Once, without warning, Jerry failed to appear at our house for a few weeks and my father sought him out to discover why. Jerry, it transpired, had begun to lose some of his hair, although he was still in his thirties. He had found a guaranteed miracle cure and, impulsively, tried it. A large pat of cow-dung, mixed with honey, had to be plastered onto his head and kept in place with a tight-fitting cap for at least two weeks. During that period, Mai slept and ate alone since Jerry was banished to the hay-barn. Unfortunately the recipe did not work. Indeed the painful removal of the encrusted mass took several locks of perfectly good, sound hair with it and left Jerry more denuded than ever.

Jerry liked a drink, though he was not addicted. However, Mai feared the influence of alcohol on him and warned all her friends that no one was to offer her husband a second drink. Jerry took a dim view of this petticoat prohibition, but pretended to go along with it. Nevertheless, outwitting her soon became a game. There were few places in our house where he could hide away safely from her observant eye, but my father aided and abetted his endeavours. Once, as I came down the stairs, I was intrigued to see a silent Mai with her ear to the bathroom door.

'What is it?' I asked. She put a finger to her lips, signalling silence. I crept closer and, sure enough, heard subdued chuckles and the chink of glasses. Mai closed her eyes in simulated despair.

'It's your father,' she whispered reproachfully, 'I just know he has Jerry in there, feeding him whiskey.'

A sheepish-looking pair emerged a little later, in great good form, and Mai darted in at once to find the offending bottle. It says something for their friendship that Mai and Dad continued to like each other, though she was a little wary of him ever after.

Jerry was a man of intense personal charm and resourcefulness. When my eldest sister and I left home to enter the Good Shepherd Convent in London, the order was strictly enclosed, so we never expected to see home again. Fourteen years later, as a result of the changes wrought by Pope John XXIII and Vatican II, we returned to Ireland for a short visit.

Our coming was a unique event. Bustling preparations, akin to the Stations, turned the house upside down. New flooring was laid, new curtains bought, and for three days, my mother and our kindly neighbours baked and roasted and planned the first splendid meal. Little nephews and nieces never before seen by us were decked out in their prettiest, frilliest clothes for our unstinted admiration. Everyone else dressed up in their Sunday best and, accompanied by such close friends as Jerry and Mai, set out for Cork airport. There, on the windswept apron, Jerry took up his position with the bagpipes. As the plane hovered over the landing strip, the haunting strains of 'Come Back To Erin' and 'You're As Welcome As The Flowers In May' rang out even to the cockpit.

Safely grounded, the whole planeload wondered what VIPs were on board as the melodies embraced them. We have had many welcomes home since then, but never again was Jerry there, trying to hide his emotion with a mischievous schoolboy grin as he folded away the pipes. He died suddenly at the wheel of his car, some years later, returning from Mass on All Saints Day. Neither Mai nor ourselves were there to say goodbye.

About a quarter of a mile below the house was the Forge. This dark and mysterious place was like a magnet for the local children. The blacksmith, known as 'Jack the Smith', was a small, balding man who lived in fire-lit semi-darkness, like a little owl. He allowed us children to creep in quietly while he worked with the heavy horses, and we watched the flared nostrils and wide, staring eyes of young colts being shod for the first time. The loud sizzling that erupted from the water butt when he plunged in a red-hot shoe, caused a great thrashing of limbs and shaking of manes and tails. Jack the Smith spoke to them soothingly, and his gentle touch soon quietened them. He was an extraordinary old man.

His artistry with horseshoes found another creative outlet. For the red-letter days in our lives, First Communion or Confirmation, Jack the Smith carved a little altar for each of us. These were mini churches painted white and gold. Inside, he made perfect little steps on which he placed a statue of Jesus or Mary. He carved the graceful silhouettes of tiny angels round the roof. Each little masterpiece was presented with great ceremony on the big day. I have mine yet.

Jack did not own his forge. He rented it from the O'Neill family, who had the small farm on which it stood. Jack had two sisters, but none of them ever married and there were no children to take over the work. Inevitably, in the fullness of time, both the sisters died and Jack, at eighty-four, became too old to work in the forge. Besides, his skills were no longer in demand as tractors were taking over. For a time, he concentrated his attention on his bees. He kept nine hives and from these generously supplied the neighbourhood with honey. He regarded the bees with awe. He firmly believed they understood every word he said. He gave them all the local news – a birth or death or a financial loss was reported to them. Once, when he had a huge swarm, he located another queen bee and decided to divide the swarm in two. He waited until evening when the bees were retiring for the night. Then he poured half of them into a newly scrubbed wooden box lined with sugar and honey. I arrived as this operation was in progress and drew back in some alarm. Jack was swathed in a black veil and long gloves.

'Come closer,' he urged me. 'They will not sting you – I've told them who you are and, besides, they're so full of honey that they are half asleep. See?' He took off his right glove and raised his hand gently, full of squirming brown bees. 'Go on,' he insisted. 'You pick them up yourself.' Holding my breath, I scooped up a pound or so of silky bees in my joined hands. It was the most extraordinary sensation, like holding live velvet that buzzed softly in the summer evening. Nervously, I jerked my hand and caught two tired bees between my fingers, but they didn't sting.

Jack was called out regularly, to cut down branches of trees on which new swarms hung. They are a rare sight these days – I suppose the new fertilisers on fields and hedgerows are not to their liking. Old Jack seemed to offer them the courtesy of a brother.

One morning, sadly, the forge was boarded up and, just like that, Jack the Smith was gone. Ballinona was a poorer place without him. My mother was full of pity for his lonely ageing friend Ned, who remained, and she made certain that a hot meal was sent to him daily. He had plenty of money but, like so many old people, he had lost the urge to cook for himself.

My sister Mary was always sent with his meal and he grew to rely on her friendliness. None of his distant relatives ever came near him until he fell seriously ill and then those with a hope of benefiting from the will came running. Suddenly he was no longer alone. Care was lavished on him, and soon solicitors and witnesses were invited to validate the will. After that, as he was inconsiderate enough to show no immediate signs of departing and all the formalities were complete, the relatives gradually left.

While his house was full of barely known visitors from distant countries, my mother had ceased her ministrations. 'Ned has no need of us now,' she told Mary. 'He has the care of his own.' When it was certain they were all gone, except one casual relative who appeared sporadically, the daily dinner was resumed. My mother accompanied Mary to see poor old Ned and note his progress.

'Ah, Mrs Moran,' he said sadly. 'You've come too late. I've settled my business but I kept this for Mary.' He reached under his pillow and produced a thick wad of money, which he insisted on giving her. My mother, who knew perfectly well it was intended for my sister Mary, nevertheless passed it over to his distant cousin, who happened to drop in that day. It was a formative incident for us. Neither of my parents would benefit themselves or allow us to benefit from the misfortunes of others. They insisted that kindness must be exercised without hope of a reward – in this world, anyway. The modern custom of charging everyone for the smallest service, from babysitting to cutting the grass, would have been anathema to their simple creed. At one point, my father always kept a spare workhorse to lend out to any local farmer who might need one.

15
Proposals

Jane Austen's opening sentence of *Pride and Prejudice* describes my next episode to perfection: 'It is a truth universally acknowledged, that a single man in possession of a large fortune, must be in want of a wife.'

George was a rich and lonely man of indeterminate age. In fact, his secrecy about his years on earth led one to suppose that he'd been around rather longer than he was prepared to admit. As well as owning an old, romantic but almost ruined castle in the south of Ireland, he'd won half a million in the Irish sweepstake. After that, there was only one area of his life in which he was visibly deprived. He had no one with whom he could share his abundant good fortune.

'George, boy,' said his friend Dick Barry, who was, by this time, my brother Joseph's father-in-law, 'You need a wife. Make no mistake about it, it's time you were married.'

George agreed, saying that he'd always intended to marry money. His boyhood dream had been to restore the dilapidated family castle. Hitherto, before the big win, the girl's looks were unimportant. She could have been as plain as a pikestaff, provided her bank balance was big enough. George was no oil painting himself, but in exchange for his name and castle, the happy girl would be allowed to spend her fortune on the house. He could then lord it, as his distant ancestors had done before him, in legendary style. Having outlined this now outmoded scheme to Dick, he continued brightly, 'Of course, all of this is no longer necessary. I have the cash now – more than I need – so I can be choosy about the wife.' The two friends lit their pipes and contemplated the problem in companionable silence.

'Well,' Dick volunteered at last, 'as I see it, you need help. Tell me your preference in the lady.'

George had a somewhat limited imagination, but he was sure of one or two angles. 'I don't want a wild one,' he said. 'She must be, er, decorative ... and ...' He went on hesitantly, 'I have servants enough, but I'd like her to have a fair knowledge of good cooking. She'll have to supervise the kitchen ... and maybe she could play cards,' he finished wistfully, 'as well as being decorative.' He was lost then in visions of his lady-love queening it as the chatelaine of his ancient seat.

Suddenly, after another prolonged pause, a bolt of lightning seemed to strike Dick. 'George!' he cried, clapping his friend on the back. 'I have the very girl for you! I know her father well. Indeed, I'm related to him by marriage. I'll see him tomorrow – no, *tonight*,' he went on enthusiastically. 'You won't want to hang around. She's well educated and decorative enough.' Warming to his theme, he began to exaggerate. 'She's a smashing cook, too, and her father will soon teach her whist. She'll pick it up in no time,' said he, disposing of any odd difficulty.

Unknown to me until much later, I was the subject of these eulogies. For reasons not unconnected with my sojourn in the convent, I had crossed the boundary line of thirty-two without accepting a husband. A few days after the above conversation, my father's somewhat sheepish approaches alerted me that something was brewing. His perturbation at my prolonged single status had become increasingly evident of late. Now there was a new, scarcely suppressed excitement in his walk and in his songs. He, who had barely smiled since my mother died, kept humming,

My singing bird,
For there's no one else can sing so sweet,
My singing bird, as you ...

Or else it would be that haunting melody 'Down by the Sally gardens, my love and I did meet.'

Eventually, with much more humming and hawing, he broke the news to me that he and Dick Barry were going to 'make a match' for me. I heard him out in dismay. It was too fantastic. I had refused more than one proposal from suitable, uninspiring men and now here was

Daddy, joyfully taking a hand in the situation himself. I didn't want to disappoint him, and I was also a little curious about the old-fashioned procedures in a vanishing ritual.

'Go ahead, Dad,' I agreed, 'but, remember, I'm unlikely to accept him.'

A week later, the date was fixed. Memories of Jim Sullivan coaching Billy flashed into my mind and I wondered if anyone was coaching George, or did he need it? A neutral house outside Midleton was chosen for the rendezvous. It was owned by a plump, cheerful widow, who looked like a pouting hen. Let's call her Bridget. This good woman was acquainted with the facts and she undertook to create a suitable social occasion with a small sherry party. About nine people, including myself, were invited. George was already there in the gloaming when I arrived with Dad and Dick Barry. They, of course, had already met and discussed practicalities, like settlements, with him. Dad told me of his love of whist. Other than that, I had refused to listen to the details of their talks, as I feared to raise Dad's expectations too high.

It was evening and a warm log fire burned brightly in the cosy but cramped sitting room. The light was fading fast. The small crowd seemed to fill the room and at first obscured 'my man', who was seated, and remained seated, by the fire in a chair that seemed too big for him. A fair amount of bright, false chat followed as I moved through the crowd. The moment I passed anyone, he or she slipped out the door, so that by the time I reached George we were alone.

Close to, I scrutinised him. One thing was for sure, he would no longer pass for forty-three in the dark with the light behind him! Indeed, when God gave out the looks, George must have been behind the door. However, he looked a peaceable enough little fellow, 'little' being the operative word. He eyed me nervously and receded even further into the winged armchair. Clouds of tobacco smoke partially obscured him. Clearly, the coaching (if he had endured it) hadn't been too productive, for at first he never said a word. Any minute now he'll produce the potatoes, I thought flippantly.

In the event, he wasn't quite so subtle. He looked to be all of fifty-six, a rather wizened gnome of a man, borne up no doubt by his money and possessions, but gauche as a schoolboy in those odd circumstances. He darted a few quick, brave glances at me, like a tortoise emerging from its shell, and then nodded to himself. I must have passed some secret test. I was a bit unsettled by this completely silent assessment and sought wildly for some everyday exchange to break the ice.

The only sounds were the comfortable crackling of the fire and the unnaturally loud ticking of the clock. Outside in the kitchen, I could hear the chink of glasses and my father's uninhibited roar of laughter. At least one part of the evening was going well.

'Good evening,' I ventured at last. 'I've been looking forward to meeting you.'

My voice seemed to galvanise him into action. He shot out of his chair and pointed the stem of his pipe at me. I was right – I topped him by two or three inches.

'Do you look to wed?' he asked bluntly, moving with surprising agility for a man of his (to me) fairly advanced years. Of course, he was a mere boy by Irish standards.

Before I could reply, he put down his pipe and came towards me, peering darkly at my hesitant self. As he moved, I noticed one of his legs was a trifle shorter than the other, giving his progress a rolling quality. Suddenly, I was speechless! How could I withdraw gracefully from this? I'll kick Dick Barry and Dad, I thought, before the night is out.

'Do you look to wed?' he repeated.

'W-well,' I half stammered, 'I'm in no rush. I thought perhaps . . .'

He turned to fetch his pipe and now stabbed the air emphatically with it. 'Well, I am. I've nothing to gain by delay, so . . .' Three flourishing stabs with the pipe stem. As proposals go, it left a little something to be desired.

'You know,' I interrupted him firmly, while striving to lighten the conversation, 'When God made time, He made plenty of it.'

'So!' He stood rooted to the ground, clearly a little nettled by my intervention. 'You're getting on a bit yourself. You wouldn't be playing with me now, would you?' he asked suspiciously.

'No – no, I'm not,' I assured him hastily. I nearly agreed to marry him in my anxiety to allay his irritation. That Dick Barry needs his ears boxed, I thought. He must have persuaded George that I was ready to leap into his arms. I went on quickly and a little sternly, 'Marriage is for the rest of my life. I have a job in London to consider. I'd have to—'

He broke in sharply at that. 'You can leave it, can't you?'

'Yes, but I'd have to give notice, make arrangements . . .' My voice trailed away a bit guiltily as a fleeting image of Mrs Bennet from *Pride and Prejudice* darted into my mind. I could hear Bridget's high-pitched voice from the kitchen. If she chose that moment to sweep in and beam her premature congratulations, before I'd extricated myself, I'd be destroyed.

'Look,' I said crisply, 'I wasn't expecting to conclude any arrangements today . . .'

A melancholy silence followed as he puffed at his pipe. It went out and he spent an agitated three minutes searching every pocket on his person for his matches. When it was alight again, he hopped along back to his chair and said, in a reflective, impersonal voice, 'Course, there's Bridget herself, the widow-woman. She's a damn good cook, I'm told.' He looked at me sourly and I grasped at straws.

'Well, I'm a hopeless cook,' I volunteered. 'I can hardly boil an egg.' This was true!

'Is that a fact?' he asked, with a hint of surprise in his voice. I think it was at that precise moment that he did a swift reappraisal of my suitability. Sensing my advantage, I went on to tell him that I couldn't play whist either and, furthermore, I disliked the smell of tobacco in a home. His face began to take on a more cheerful expression that bordered on relief at his escape.

Clearly, I was a real 'wild one', with no proper sense of gratitude for the honour being offered to me. He even relaxed enough to offer me a thimbleful of Bristol Cream sherry in a tiny Waterford glass. Then we sat down together to discuss his rheumatism and the poor eyesight of his dog. When the others sidled in, they looked coy at first and later disappointed.

We parted amicably enough and he probably forgot me the moment I was over the threshold. For my part, I'd already met the man who would become my future husband over in England. He proved to be one in a million when I subsequently married him. My father, too, once he recovered from his initial disappointment, welcomed an English son-in-law with an approval that was cautious at first, but later wholehearted.

16

A Polite and Generous People

In recent years, the British media refers with insufferable frequency to 'mainland Britain'. By implication, the island of Ireland seems to be a nondescript little place, achieving its limited importance solely from its geographical position to the west of Britain. Many Irish people find this lofty smugness a bit disconcerting. Mainland Ireland, too, goes back a long way. It has never colonised others, never imposed its culture by force and never displaced any other nation. Overall, it has offered friendliness and humour to the world, as well as dignity and grace in times of suffering.

Pope Pius XII once said, 'The Irish are like the presence of God – they're everywhere.'

It is a characteristic of the British that they tend to distance themselves from whatever threatens them by making fun of it. Humour is a splendid way of getting life into perspective and the British are quite brilliant at this. As a result of this liberally applied technique, many Irish in Britain find it hard to pass on their culture and history to their English-born children. At school, in the media or on the high street, the image of the thick, easily duped Irishman is a powerful and enduring image. Where I sang 'O'Donnell Abu' and dreamed of 'The Wild Geese of Tirconnel',[3] my children imagined illiterate men keeping pigs in the kitchen. These entrenched attitudes, shaped by a thousand years of history, are being challenged today. A new generation of bright, confident Irish youngsters, technologically aware and fluent in many languages, is now flooding Britain's businesses and universities,

3 The Earls of the North who were forced into exile in the days of Elizabeth I.

as well as those on the Continent. Slight shock waves at their erudition and self-assurance are beating hard against age-old prejudices.

My own experience of the Irish I knew is that they are the politest people in the world. They have a sensitivity and courtesy that obliges strangers to be vigilant, lest they inadvertently take an unfair advantage.

Two examples from my youth, of their good manners and neighbourliness, will remain with me always. One occurred in my father's old age, when he was alone in Brookedale and was trying to keep it solvent almost by himself. He needed many planks of wood to repair the cow byres. As luck would have it, a recent heavy storm had brought down a suitable tree. It lay across the lawn field, heavy and unwieldy and quite impossible for a man of Daddy's age to manage alone. One fine day, after I'd come home on holiday, my father announced that the tree must be taken to the sawmill. So familiar was I with the helpfulness of Ballinona's community that I saw no problem either.

Dad and I brought the saw and axes and walked down to the tree. Then I stepped out of the gates and stopped every car, cart and bicycle until we had about nine men. Not one of them hesitated or refused. Once they understood that their brawn and brain were needed, they parked their transport where they could, rolled up their sleeves and set to work. An hour or so later, the enormous trunk was denuded of all its branches and sawn into three large, heavy sections.

The next step was to get those tons of wood to the sawmill. Young Dennis Hennessey, a friendly farmer who had a day's harvesting lined up, instantly shelved his plans and went home for his tractor and trailer. The lawn field ended at a stone wall, about six feet above the road. It was necessary to line up the trailer with the field, then roll the great logs towards it. The workers, our local Justice of the Peace among them, fell to with crowbars and manoeuvred the sections of trunk down to the trailer. In their enthusiasm, they let the first one go too quickly and it fell with an explosive thump. It cracked a hole about a foot wide in the flooring. Dennis looked at it critically and said, 'OK, boys! I can soon replace that – the axle is all right. Push in the next one.'

He then drove at least six miles to Killeagh sawmills with his load. In those days, countrymen took each other's goodness for granted.

When Dennis had gone, all the others came in for tea and the gathering soon developed into a mini-party. In no time John-Joe, the JP, was persuaded to sing 'Genevieve' to a tune all his own, and whatever affairs the others were going about originally were calmly put off until the next day. No wonder I loved them all!

Perhaps my most poignant memory on this theme occurred at my father's last birthday party. About eighty friends turned up. There was a quartet of local musicians, led by Mack Cotter, whose skills as a violinist lifted that evening and many another into his own realm of harmony. My father was in his element. He looked forward to a uniquely Irish night, stretching way into the small hours with scores of friends singing, drinking and reminiscing. By one thirty in the morning, the jollifications showed no sign of abating. I had to leave the next day, more or less as the dawn broke, as I was catching an early ferry. When my father put down his flute and retired briefly to the bathroom about 2 a.m., I grasped the opportunity to explain to our guests that my departure was imminent. I had been away from them for years and I can only think now that my sensibilities had become blunted.

'Listen, everybody!' I said, getting a moment of quiet. 'I want to thank you all for coming. I have to leave very early tomorrow, so I'm going to get a few hours of sleep. I expect some of you are a little tired yourselves, so I'll say goodnight and thanks again.' Somehow, this clumsy speech conveyed an unintentional note of dismissal. Almost before I could blink, every man, woman and musician stood up, finished their drinks and were going out the door when my amazed father emerged from the bathroom.

'Where are you all going?' he inquired in astonishment. 'The night is still young!'

' 'Tis time we were off, Con,' they replied politely and, I thought, evasively. With that, they vanished like snow in summer.

I didn't dare tell Dad how ham-fisted I'd been. I'd just forgotten the fine sensitivity of these friends of my youth. As I've said, it was a last party, so I didn't meet them again until his funeral.

This courtesy is, for me, the authentic stamp of the Celt. When I read that Sidney Reilly, the 'Ace of Spies' and famous Russian agent, chose his Irish surname because he wanted to be accepted primarily as a gentleman, it confirmed all my own early conclusions about the gracious good manners which marked so many I knew well.

They were even polite to God. In a Youghal pub one Thursday night at 11.55 p.m., our party was served roast chicken with our drinks. Someone spotted the time. 'Hey!' he said. 'It's almost midnight – 'twill soon be Friday and then we'll be breaking the fast.'[4]

There was a minute's wondering silence. Then one lad stood up and crossed over to the clock. 'He won't mind,' he said, pointing upwards. Then he turned the clock back to 11 p.m. 'Eat away, lads,' he said. 'You're all right now.' People reached for the chicken legs again, never doubting that God was on our side.

---

4 Catholics were obliged then to fast from eating meat on Fridays – until Vatican II cancelled the custom.

PART TWO

I

Those Convent Days

'There's a Divinity that shapes our ends, rough-hew them
how we will' *Hamlet*

The war was over in 1945 and oranges came to Ireland for the first
time. In their wake came all manner of changes. Taoiseach Éamon de
Valera's stature was greatly enhanced as it became obvious that he
had won his duel with Churchill over the ports. His refusal to let the
Allies use them – maintaining Ireland's neutrality – had the full support of a people long tired of bloodshed, and unaware then of the full
evil threat to our civilisation that the Nazis represented. We too settled down to the business of growing up. A local family lost their
mother in a tragic accident and for the first time, at her funeral, when
I saw the grieving, untidy children, accompanied by their bewildered,
helpless father, I understood the bleakness of the word 'orphan'.

I was full of compassion. With a shiver, my childish mind envis-
aged a similar situation and leaped ahead to the double loss of both
parents. Where would such children go and who would care for them?
Aunty Josie answered my endless questions. In Ireland, at that time,
orphanages were mainly set up by nuns – there being no state provision. Instantly, I saw this as a very worthwhile activity. I thought, in
my green years, that teaching and nursing nuns led a somewhat uninspiring existence, but caring for lonely, deprived children was, for me,
a most attractive idea.

Shortly after my fourteenth birthday, when the wintry sun of
November cast a cold eye over my school classroom, an early bell

summoned all of us into a general assembly. The harassed Leaving
Certificate class was already there, looking relieved that the pressure
of work was lifted from them even briefly. We were told that we had
two distinguished visitors from England. Soon the principal ushered
in two stately nuns dressed in white. First came a rather stern, tall nun
called Mother St Kevin. She had that aura of authority about her
which Jung calls 'numen'. When she spoke, even very quietly, we
strained to hear. With her was her natural sister, Mother Mary of Our
Lady. She had the lesser role. She was tall, attractive and energetic. Of
the two, she was more articulate and imaginative. By no means a
dreamer, she could quote poetry with a fluency that denoted a sensitive classical education. I was to get to know her well, and one of her
proudest stories was of how as a young girl she had known and liked
the ageing and forgetful G. K. Chesterton.

The nuns told us of their work for the poor and deprived – especially
for girls and women in some of the big cities of postwar Britain.
School was not very exciting anyway and seemed to stretch along a
grey road ahead for years and years. Imagining myself as an angel of
mercy gathering up and comforting broken-hearted children seemed a
much more enticing prospect.

Straight away, I offered myself as a trainee. Though they baulked
initially at my green youth, they gave a provisional acceptance. My
older sister Mauraid, studying for her Leaving Certificate with university beckoning, also volunteered and renounced her plans.

Excitedly we cycled home, eager to impart the news to our parents.
To our delight, we spotted Dad driving towards us in the trap. We
barred his progress with our bicycles. How raw and immature we
were, blissfully unaware of the blow we were about to deliver to him!
Half his family gone in one fell swoop!

'Daddy!' we chorused. 'We are going over to England next week to
be nuns.'

He blanched visibly, knowing far better than we did the enormity
of what we were suggesting. Laughing and shouting, we began to tell
him what we knew, while he listened in dismay. Beneath all his banter,
he had a strong religious faith, which was deep and abiding. He knew
something of the ways of the world and perhaps he saw security for

us. Finally, he flicked the reins on the horse and said the words I shall never forget, 'If God wants you, I will not stand in your way,' and his horse broke into a trot. I can see him now, sitting square behind that horse, his hat pressed firmly down over his forehead and all song dead on his lips.

Slightly sobered, we continued home and electrified our mother and Aunty Josie with our news. For the first few days, they were in a state of suspended disbelief. But the nuns sent for them, pointing out it was not final and promising that our education would be completed. In my case, they assured my parents that I would come home once more before I entered the Noviciate – the training. I too was told this, and so for me it was a great adventure into the unknown. Of course, after the mysterious Noviciate, there would be another three years before any kind of commitment was made permanent.

So it was decided, and joyously we entered into the spirit of the occasion. We were giving our lives to God and following the Gospel precepts. First of all, we had to follow the directive: 'If you will be perfect, go sell what you have and give to the poor. Then come follow Me.'

I gave my school bicycle to my brother Joseph. With the only tinge of regret during the whole business, I parted with my box of costume jewellery to be shared amongst my school friends. As I was still a schoolgirl, I took my best clothes with me. My mother, in tears, made me a pretty, dark green suit, the last garment she ever made for me.

Carried along in a surge of excitement, Mauraid and I decided to give a farewell party. My parents decreed that twenty or thirty people would be enough. In fact, we invited over a hundred and they all came! It was like a cross between a wake and a wedding. Of course, as at every Irish party, everyone sang. Until well into the small hours, the rafters roared with the familiar songs of our childhood. I remember vividly the surging enthusiasm as the packed crowd joined in 'The Star of the County Down', followed by the proud and plaintive 'Boulavogue'. To these, 'The Wild Rover' and 'The Mountains of Mourne', our family song, took second place because ten minutes after every new song someone in the packed crowd called out, 'Con, give us "Boulavogue" again.'

For the last time, I sat on a young man's knee as he sang softly to me: 'I can't begin to tell you, dear, how much you mean to me.' Later that night, that young man asked my *sister* to give up all idea of being a nun and instead to stay at home and marry him! I fear he had a roving eye and a fickle heart! We finished the party as the darkness fled, and with the Guinness all gone, Dad played 'I'll Take You Home Again, Kathleen' to an almost silent crowd.

We left home heavily laden on 30 November. Half the neighbourhood came to wave us off and generous were the blessings and good advice. Many pressed money on us and half-crowns and two-shilling pieces were slipped into our pockets. 'Take it for the journey,' they whispered.

My well-to-do American friend, whose babies and trunks I had once rescued from the flooded river, gave me five pounds, which was a fortune. 'Hide it in your bra,' she advised my flat-chested self, who had not yet started to wear one. So I slipped it up the leg of my sensible knickers instead.

Mam and Dad came with us to the first stop, a Cork City convent. They were proud and anxious, accepting the mores of our society and, I suppose, relieved at one level that we would henceforth be protected from the 'slings and arrows of outrageous fortune'. Dry-eyed, I hugged them at parting.

We were conducted to a spartan dormitory. There, we were warned to be silent, and soon the lights went out. I remember I pulled the sheets over my head and thought dismally, Lord, what have I done?

At six the next morning, we were startled out of sleep by a vigorously rung bell. In no time at all, we were crowded onto a ship bound for England. There were ten of us and just two quiet nuns. As the ship pulled out of the harbour, taking us away from the life we had known, I looked back at the shifting light on the hills behind the city and I thought of the words of the Irish poet John Locke:

> There it is, the dawn on the hills of Ireland,
>   God's angels lifting the night's black veil,
>   From the fair sweet face of my Sireland.

Dad had called us both into his bedroom before we left and, with barely concealed emotion and a solemnity quite foreign to him, said, 'Remember that while I live, you will always have a home here.'

Many years later, long after he died, I returned alone to find another family in residence.[5] They said it was inconvenient for me to come inside, as they were eating. As I walked back down the avenue, I was unexpectedly choked with emotion. The lovely words of my grandfather came back to me: 'You have nothing to be afraid of here, with the souls of all your ancestors thick as bees around you.'

The writer of 'Round the Boree Log' expressed the loss of his old home in different words:

> There a stranger has her evenings
> and the formal supper's spread
> but I wonder has she Trimmings now
> and is the Rosary said.

5 After his death in '75 and my brother's death the following year, Brookedale was briefly rented out to a young South African couple.

2

New Beginnings

On 2 December 1946, we arrived at our London convent in icy darkness. Tired but expectant, we were shown immediately to our dormitory. Each of us had a small, spotlessly clean space curtained off from the rest. It held a narrow white bed and a chest of drawers with a jug and basin. On the wall was a little brown crucifix. Thankfully, we fell into our respective beds and slept. Seconds later, or so it seemed to me, we were awakened. It was still dark and the lights came on down the centre of the dormitory. A small rotund nun crept silently in and whispered, 'Put on your black dress and wait.' Of course, I did not have a black dress as I was to go to school.

'Never mind,' she whispered. 'I'll get you something.'

Now I may have been bursting with noble notions, but I still had a teenager's healthy interest in clothes. In a short time, the Sister glided back and handed me a long, oblong garment without shape or make to it. As mirrors were a forbidden luxury, I could only judge the ghastly effect when I saw the others giggling.

By then, it was 6.30 a.m. and old songs from the dawn chorus began to drift in. With great emphasis on quiet, we were escorted into an adjoining room where pretty white bonnets covered in shoulder-length black netting were presented to each of us. This was almost the last time I was to see my sister, and indeed most of the others, with their hair uncovered. The exceptions were the three other youngsters who were to go out to school.

It must have been a proud moment for the community of nuns when the ten of us, like young blackbirds, trooped into the chapel that first morning. The tall, vaulted building was quite beautiful: high stained-glass windows glowed in colour and all of the nuns (about forty of them) were dressed in white in choir stalls which faced the altar. Several wore the white veils of Novices – the others wore black ones.

Stalls? I thought irreverently. Do they think we're calves? The nuns sang Prime, a selection from the psalms, in clear sweet voices, their faces serene and happy, their eyes downcast.

After Mass, we were directed through broad cloisters to the refectory where all the Sisters stood in silence to drink scalding tea and eat bread and butter. Awed by the pervading silence, we, too, kept quiet and we were soon conducted to the Noviciate.

This was a huge, somewhat comfortless room. Eight enormously high windows overlooked a drab winter garden. The Noviciate was furnished with a twenty-foot table down one side and about fifty chairs lining the other wall. An enormous bookcase filled one corner. It was always locked except when the Novice Mistress opened it to distribute *Lives of the Saints* and other books she considered suitable for our spiritual development.

Sister Rose, the Deputy Novice Mistress, explained the rules. No casual or social gossip was to be indulged in throughout the day. We were to observe absolute silence, with just two exceptions. After lunch, from 12.30 to 1.30, we could sit and talk and laugh while we sewed, and again for an hour after the evening meal.

That togetherness was also very carefully defined. We were warned that we must avoid all particular friendships. The whole group sat in a circle round the Novice Mistress but we were told not to sit more than twice beside the same person. When we walked in the garden we were to do so in threes. Certain topics were forbidden. Like Melchisedec in the Book of Genesis, we presented ourselves without antecedents – at least, none we could talk about. Our homes, our relatives and our former way of life were never to be mentioned. Even our surnames were to be secret. It was as though our lives began the day we arrived. We heard of a girl who was told at the convent door: 'Remember to leave your own will on the outside.'

'He wasn't Will, he was Jim,' she replied, grinning.

That very first day we were told of the importance of yet another kind of silence. This was the 'Great Silence'. It began at 9 p.m. and finished after Mass at about eight the next morning.

'It is a time of special quiet, a time to pray about the many bad things that happen in the world at night,' said Sister Mary Rose. The nuns always referred to the 'world' as if it were another planet. Actually, did she but know it, we hadn't a clue about bad things in the world, coming as most of us did, from a very sheltered Irish country background.

We were told to observe the Great Silence by walking quietly, by opening and closing doors without making a sound, using both hands if necessary. Above all, we were to wear soft felt slippers called 'Silent Shoes'. Of course we didn't talk or rattle any objects. If urgent communication was needed, we wrote a note.

Each of us was given a lined sewing basket and many numbered tags. Every article of clothing was to be marked and stockings were to be further marked with long tapes so that they could be tied together for the laundry. 'Always tie your stockings together,' insisted Sister Mary Rose. Clearly, one of us was overwhelmed by the multitude of directives and must have caught only snippets. Next morning she was observed coming down the stairs in little hops and looking quite embarrassed.

'What's the matter?' one of us asked, though the stairs was a place on which you weren't supposed to talk.

'I don't know how the rest of you manage,' she replied, 'but I cannot get up and down those stairs with the tops of my stockings tied together!'

3
Early Mornings

The name for a trainee is 'postulant' and soon I had a new identity. I became known as a 'school postulant'. As such, I was allowed a rest in the mornings so I arose half an hour after the others, at 6.30 a.m. At this Godly hour, I donned the long, plain black dress and bonnet and went to Mass. At 8.15, I returned to the outer rooms and changed into school uniform: light blue blouse and belted navy gymslip. Three other school postulants did the same.

From there we set off for the local grammar school where none of the other pupils knew we were going to be nuns. They did, however, find certain aspects of our garb confusing. When summer arrived, the whole school changed into silky blue dresses and white ankle socks instead of the heavy black stockings. After some deliberation, we were allowed the dresses but were forbidden the less modest ankle socks. I didn't mind this until a kindly girl in my class took me aside and said if I couldn't afford the socks she would give me a pair of hers. I think the other pupils thought we came from a convent orphanage. As my mother had been regarded as the neighbourhood Lady Bountiful, I found this image of myself, as an object needing charity, more than disconcerting. I refused with unnecessary sharpness, thus losing her friendship.

We were encouraged to join in every school activity except swimming. This was considered far too risqué for budding nuns. In fact, there was a somewhat medieval attitude to baths in our convent. We were allowed thirty minutes once a week in the locked bathroom. There, we were instructed to wear bath chemises. These consisted of two full lengths of white calico sewn together at the shoulders, which could be slipped over our heads so that we were covered back and front. In the bath they billowed and floated over us as we washed. No perfumed soap was allowed. Instead we used hard, carbolic soap. I suppose the idea was to stop us admiring our young bodies. Such vanity was no threat to me because at that time I resembled a stick insect, but I scrubbed myself clean under a wet tent like all the others.

My mother had voiced several concerns about life in the convent. I remember her asking a bit timidly if they had fires. 'Kathleen suffers from the cold,' she said. She was assured that all the convents had modern central heating. This was true of the ground floor, but right up at the top of the third storey there was neither heat nor running water. Our washing jugs were frozen solid each winter morning. However, the ice was thin and easily broken and none of us minded much the splash of cold which sent sleep flying.

For an age, I longed for more sleep. Indeed I began to think that Heaven was a place of peaceful, uninterrupted sleep where raucous rattles could not penetrate. Each of the older nuns took a turn at calling us. She would arise at 5.30 a.m. and knock loudly on each door saying, 'Blessed be God.' Then she waited for the sleepy or lively reply, 'Deo gratias!' God be thanked. 'Get out of bed as if it was on fire,' we were admonished if we were slow. In the glad morning of our days, we tried, we really tried.

No one was forcing us to stay there, and as the months passed, we gained some little understanding of this unusual and challenging way of life. The Sisters behaved like real sisters and they were invariably kind to us. They saw us as the Order's future and sought to develop whatever small talents we possessed. We were sent to bed at 9 p.m., and in the light spring evenings, I found it difficult to settle into the spirit of the Great Silence.

One evening, I decided to liven things up a little. I took the sheet off my bed and wrapped it round me. Quietly, I crept into the shadows at the top of the stairs and stood there moaning as the other school postulants came up to bed. With a piercing shriek, Sister Joan was the first to see me. She took off like a bullet, but the others twigged who I was and descended on me, laughing and giggling. I ran. We thought we had the dormitory to ourselves because the community were in church far away from us, saying night prayers.

To escape my pursuers and hampered by the trailing sheet, I dashed into an old Sister's room. To my horror, I heard a groan from the bed behind me, as I listened to their running feet outside. I stood stock still and heard barely suppressed sounds of 'Jesus, Mary and Joseph!' The incredulous eyes of old Sister Marcus stared at me. She blinked and started to struggle up as I moved to her doorway curtain and backed out. She raised a trembling hand and made the sign of the Cross into the air. 'Go back to where you came from, in the name of God,' she said weakly.

I slipped into my own dormitory, which was nearby. There I waited, scarcely breathing as I listened for developments. I was lucky – perhaps she'd thought I was a figment of a dream rather than a visitation from another world. I never found out her conclusions because professed nuns were not allowed to speak to postulants. My friends waited to talk about it until we were on our way to school the next day. We never did that again.

The week after our arrival in the convent, two more girls arrived, from Ulster. Both of them came to school with us and remarked on how refreshing it was to attend a known Catholic school without jeers and name-calling. The Troubles of a later time had not yet started, but the sectarian divide was well established.

More young vocations came from month to month. One contingent came from Malta: two very young, charming girls and one rather ample lady named Sister Helen, in her late twenties. Sister Helen was about sixteen or seventeen stone and moved in majestic stateliness through the cloisters. I was sent to escort her upstairs to the dormitory. She could not speak any English but her expressive face soon showed her clear disapproval of her narrow bed. She sniffed audibly several times, felt the mattress and even thumped it dismissively. She graced me then with a fluent stream of indignant Maltese.

Helplessly, I backed away and ran downstairs. In that place of self-denial, I never dreamed of passing on her reservations about the accommodation to the Novice Mistress. We were meant to welcome little inconveniences as opportunities to grow in grace.

Soon after nine o'clock that night, pandemonium broke out in our quiet dormitory. Loud groans, thrashing about and rusty creaks emanated from Sister Helen's curtained cubicle. The Great Silence forgotten, we all rushed in to investigate. Sister Helen had fallen through the springs of her frail bed and, struggle as she would, she could not dislodge herself. Her little fat legs were waving high in the air while her rear end was stuck right through the middle. Her arms and angry red face were pinned at the pillow end. The more she struggled, the more deeply enmeshed she became. The air around her was full of Maltese expletives, which we naturally translated into prayers to all the saints. Six of us endeavoured to drag her out, but the bed frame came with her. Hunched double and fairly choking with rage, she staggered with it across the dormitory. We were helpless with laughter by then and no use to anyone.

When she reached our dormitory door, still encased in the bent bed frame, she could not get through to leave us. She had to be carefully manoeuvred sideways so one of us could go for help.

The Infirmarian and two strong, sensible nuns, one with wirecutters, soon arrived. Sister Helen was released and given a mattress on the floor for the rest of the night. She went home to Malta the next day.

The Mistress of Novices was a stern and rather grim lady. She seemed to keep a wary eye on me in particular and I tried to bring myself to her attention as rarely as possible. Once, either at school or in the changing rooms at the convent, I managed to lose the navy belt of my gymslip. This was in the nature of a catastrophe. I couldn't possibly appear at school with my uniform billowing about me, so I had to tell her. As expected, she hit the roof. How could I *possibly* think of taking a vow of poverty when I could not even look after my clothes? And this wasn't the only thing! Wasn't I seen *running* up the cloister only yesterday? All sorts of infringements were lodged in her prodigious memory. I resolved to do better and avoid future encounters. I was given a new belt, but to my unimaginable dismay, I lost it again three weeks later. It was on a Friday evening so I had the weekend to consider the matter. Where could I get another belt without more strictures and black marks?

The far end of our dormitory had been sectioned off as a storeroom. The solid partition stopped about three feet from the ceiling.

I knew that all the luggage we had brought from home was lodged in there. In mine was the navy gymslip I used to wear to Midleton High School, but how to get it? The door to the storeroom was always locked and only the Novice Mistress had the key. As I lay in bed cogitating on my dilemma, I looked up at the ceiling and noticed that two large hot-water pipes ran the full length of the dormitory. They were about eight inches in diameter and I was young and athletic. I knew I could do it. I saw I would have to wait until the still watches of the night when all the Sisters in their cubicles would be sound asleep. Once I was up on the pipes (with the aid of a chair) I would have to hang above their heads and pray they wouldn't open their eyes.

I set myself to wait. Slowly the hours passed and all restless rustlings ceased. I began to feel like Lady Macbeth: 'One, two – why then, 'tis time to do't!'

I positioned the chair carefully and made a silent leap, hoping the hot pipe would be bearable. It was. I skimmed along above the heads of three Sisters, a mere shadow in the night. I dropped safely down on the other side of the partition and, with stealthy care, took down the piled trunks until I recognised my own in the semi-darkness. Only the glimmerings of the central dormitory red light penetrated the storeroom. Eventually my fumbling fingers found my belt. Despite an ominous creak from the rusty pipes, I safely regained the sanctuary of my cubicle. Next morning, I examined my belt. To my intense dismay, I discovered it was green! The next day, to my secret amusement, my friend Sister Bridie remarked that she'd had a dream about me the night before. 'You seemed to be flying along the ceiling!'

It must be remembered that these episodes of light entertainment passed side by side with serious efforts to train us for our new roles. Our own spirituality was deepened with lectures, books and retreats. Our youth made us both vulnerable and idealistic.

I related easily to stories of exciting saints. Our Novice Mistress told us that there is no such thing as a hidden saint because sanctity is too rare to be overlooked. In particular, I liked Saint Elizabeth of Hungary. As a girl, younger than I was, she left her native Thuringia to become engaged to the young King of Hungary. She married him at the age of sixteen and was completely happy until he went on the Crusades, where he was killed. His mother then threw her out of the palace and made no provision for her. She was forced to work as a servant for a cranky old man until her husband's men returned. Fulfilling a promise they had made to the dying king, to protect and serve his queen, they sought her out and reinstated her. Not once did she grumble or rail against her fate, but accepted her changing circumstances with peace and serenity as the will of God.

Step by step, we were taught meditation and prayer, to be at peace and relax, to stop striving for immediate goals. We were told to empty our minds of all distractions and listen instead to God.

My father used to tell a story of a man who greatly coveted a farmer's handsome horse. One day, he told the farmer that he would give anything to own such a fine animal. The farmer replied, 'Well, it's quite easy. If you can say the Lord's Prayer all the way through without a distraction, I will give you my horse.'

'Done,' said the man. He shut his eyes and began aloud: 'Our Father, Who art in Heaven, hallowed be Thy Name. Thy kingdom come . . .' He opened his eyes and said, 'Will you give me the saddle and bridle too?'

The farmer took his horse and rode away, chuckling.

4

The Fledgling Nun

For eighteen months of our training we had nothing to do with the Sisters' youngest charges. We were considered far too undignified and worldly to be entrusted with the care of little ones. The Novice Mistress had a special word for me – flippant. My whole attitude had too much flippancy about it, so she said. Balanced people, I was told, had a sense of both gravitas and humour, but she decided all my humour turned out to be mere flippancy. Even so, on one occasion, even her grave demeanour melted, just a touch.

We had been in silent retreat for eight days. The silence was absolute. We read holy books and we listened to wise sermons. We meditated on our readiness to commit ourselves to this life of dedication. It was summer time and the gardens were ablaze with flowers and apple blossom. We found our own quiet corners, well away from others, and contemplated amid the bird song, the life ahead of us and the step we were about to take. As Wordsworth wrote, 'Bliss it was in that dawn to be alive – but to be young was very heaven!'

At the end of eight days, we were to be dressed in long white bridal dresses and lace veils, which swept down to the floor. Hair was washed and shampooed and set in the most becoming styles we knew. We were all in our late teens and I suppose we never looked better, both happy and excited. The day before the Clothing ceremony, as it was called, when we would receive the habit of the Order, the solemn Novice Mistress took us down for a rehearsal. The peaceful church was very quiet and she trooped us up to Reverend Mother's empty chair to bow politely and offer her the kiss of peace.

There were sixty empty places for absent Sisters, whom we would greet the next day. I might have survived one such miming encounter, but we had to practise greeting each one. After eight days of absolute quiet, I might also have been a bit light-headed. Suddenly the image of myself bowing deeply to empty places, kissing the air around imaginary persons, struck me as being inexpressibly funny. The experience was like laughing gas and it was infectious. All nine of us grew weak from suppressed laughter and we were swaying about quite unable to finish the rehearsal. For once the very serious Novice Mistress understood and actually smiled herself. A stranger glancing into that gem of a church would have been astounded to see the nine of us convulsed with merriment in that sacred place.

The next day was beautiful. It was spring in 1951. My mother and father came from Ireland and were moved to tears by the sight of us – nine fledgling nuns. Afterwards my father sat in the convent parlour and played on the flute: 'Come Back To Erin, Mavourneen' and, ironically, 'I'll Take You Home Again, Kathleen'. We knew and they knew that at that point we could return home any time we liked. Though I had some doubts even at that early stage, I wanted to continue to try out the work of caring for the needy when my turn came.

After the Clothing event and my First Vows, there were three years to come before I would have to decide whether to make my Final Vows.

A poem I wrote years later sums up the glad idealism of those days:

> How can I capture now
> The light and laughter of those bygone years?
> Vignettes of life – the music, the white veil,
> The glory of the chapel and my Holy Grail,
> Receptive and innocent, we sought ideals,
> And love of God came chasing at our heels.
> Subtle beauties found us, bound us,
> The camaraderie – the silent peace,
> The growing wonder that His caring never ceased.
> Tentatively – alert to hurt – I sought Him in the images He made.
> So many of my friends reflected Him
> And in their gladness I could trace
> The contours of His Human Face.

During those formative years, I had some extraordinary experiences. I was introduced to a world where parents rejected and neglected their children; I met young people so damaged by man's inhumanity to man that their psyches had almost disintegrated. The policy of the Sisters was to be invariably kind to them, to find goals for them to achieve – to give them a sense of success so that their self-images would grow into lifelong maturity. The Foundress of the Good Shepherd Order, a French saint, had laid down some very strict and wise rules for the care of children. They must never, but never, we were told, be slapped or ill-treated in any way. Many were used to violence: the only role-models they had were cruel and abusive. In contrast, the nuns had to be full of compassion and patience.

5
Tragedy and Love

Half a dozen individual girls' histories will stay in my memory for ever. In this account, I have changed their names, omitted the places where I met them, but I think even my short-lived and limited experience illustrates the Herculean task the Sisters undertook. I use the word 'Sisters' advisedly because that was what they were. I knew them well – we grew up together. We talked of our hopes and fears, our ideals and our helplessness without the Grace of God to bind up the wounded and heal the sick and broken.

One fifteen-year-old runaway was committed to us through the courts for being beyond control. The judge berated her for lying about her father, just to get his attention, he supposed. The father held an honourable profession and was highly regarded in his community. His evidence was that she had been manipulative and deceitful and rebellious since her mother died. The hearts of all in the court were touched as the man described his endeavours to be mother and father at the same time to a thankless child. The convent school headmistress was full of sympathy for the poor man. He accompanied the girl – I will call her Jenny – to our 'special school'. In the main, the ordinary staff knew nothing of the girls' past experiences but Sister Agnes obliquely warned us to be alert to the wiles of young Jenny. She was quiet as a lamb, never smiled and made no friends. Sister Agnes suspected that it was a case of 'still waters run deep'.

One month after her arrival, her father, boisterous and drunk, came to see her. She refused to go near him, and Sister Agnes again expressed her sympathy for the unfortunate father. To her astonishment, he laughed in her face. 'Oh, come on, Sister,' he said. 'Surely you didn't believe all that baloney. Jenny was telling the truth but usually it was when I was drunk . . .' Sister Agnes was speechless with disgust.

As I had some counselling training by this time, I was asked to offer Jenny some help. Obviously the whole can of worms could be reopened in the courts and Jenny was free to leave. This she refused to do, begging to be allowed to stay in the only place where she felt safe. She was like a bird with a broken wing, and the Sisters cared for her with endless compassion. They educated her and she took her School Certificate in six subjects with merits. After she left, she visited the convent again and again, coming first with her fiancé, then her husband and eventually two children. The nuns had created for her a bridge to normality and decency.

Then there was Eileen Langley who came to us through the courts at the age of fifteen, accused of truanting. She too was reckoned by the social workers to be beyond control. Eileen was small, dark-eyed and pretty. She never settled. Despite the activities organised for the girls – plays, games and concerts – Eileen avoided participation and instead wandered round wearing a perpetually anxious expression. She reacted to attempts at friendliness like a startled deer, backing off and looking hostile. However, when she grew more trusting, she told me that the only reason she had played truant was to protect her mother from her violent father. She lived in fear that in her absence her mother might suffer some unspeakable horror.

Her fears were justified one cold January day. A social worker came to break the news that her beloved mother had been murdered in a savage beating at the hands of her father. Eileen was so stricken that she could not speak. Head bowed and white-faced, she walked out with the social worker to give evidence at the trial. She never returned. Her father was given a life sentence and her three brothers and sisters were sent to different care homes. So the whole family was scattered. I heard later that, when Eileen was eighteen, she applied for the release of the younger family members into her care. The Sisters, with their endless concern and sympathy, helped her to set up home with them.

Not every story was as tragic as Eileen's. One beautiful girl called May left the school and found a job in the local hotel. Among the guests was a young American who asked her to have dinner with him on her evening off. She liked him, thought him very handsome and charming, and agreed to see him again. He fell in love with her and, for the next few months, wined and dined her all over the city. When he asked her to marry him, she said she would like to take him to the convent first. She relied completely on the judgement of the headmistress, who had helped her so much.

Sister Beatrice fully approved of him – and plans were made for the wedding in the convent chapel. As his family were all in the States, she was told she would meet them later. Straight after the ceremony they flew out to New York. A chauffeur-driven limousine met them at the airport. She teased him about the prodigality of hiring such a luxurious car, but he only laughed and said she was worth it. After driving for some hours the car turned in through impressive white gates and began a long journey up the drive. Soon they reached a beautiful gabled cottage and she inquired breathlessly if that was theirs.

'No,' he replied. 'Ours is further on.'

She thought he looked a little uneasy. To her amazement, round the next bend she saw an incredibly attractive mansion. She assumed they would drive past it, but slowly the car came to a halt.

Outside, there were about a dozen people all waving and smiling. Most of them were in neat, black dresses and white aprons. At the front were a dignified old lady and gentleman. The young husband leaped out and hugged them. 'Meet my bride,' he said happily, as he put an arm round her and drew her forward.

May was speechless with surprise. Over a vast reception banquet in an elegant dining room, he explained to her that all his life, predatory mamas had pursued him as an eligible husband for their daughters. He explained that he was always uncertain about their effusive declarations of love since he was known to be the richest young man in the county. At least with May he was sure that she was not marrying him for his money.

Some stories are more heart-wrenching. There was a mayor of a city in Canada whose family was so prestigious and wealthy that the city hall had to be hired to accommodate and display his daughter's wedding gifts. Alice was his only child and she was set to inherit her father's vast estates. Adjoining those estates was another huge expanse of prairie land owned by the neighbouring Cornwallis family. This family had even greater social status. They, too, had an only child, a son. It seemed obvious to the parents that a match should be made between the two youngsters. So, from a very early age, Alice knew that her life was mapped out for her. She liked the boy and he liked her, but they actually saw very little of each other as they grew up. Both went to boarding schools and were taken abroad during the holidays. Their engagement was announced even so, when Alice was eighteen. The rejoicing was city wide.

Secretly, and unknown to any member of her family, Alice had fallen in love with a local delivery boy. She began to see him regularly and one frightening morning she realised that she was pregnant. Of course she had to tell her mother, who was horrified. They were Catholics, so there was no question of an abortion. Her mother decided to hide her in their country house seventy miles outside the city. Only her nanny went with her, and her mother announced to all and sundry that, unfortunately, Alice had contracted an embarrassing skin rash on her face. The doctors were treating it, but by her own wish no visitors were allowed.

The family doctor was in attendance and after a long and difficult labour, Alice was delivered of a baby boy. Exhausted after the birth, Alice fell into a deep, prolonged sleep while the nanny took care of the baby. Several hours later, when Alice awoke, her mother came to her in tears. 'The baby did not make it, darling,' she said. 'I'm very sorry.' While Alice was disappointed, she accepted the loss and, in the end, agreed with her mother that perhaps it was all for the best and the grand wedding could now go ahead.

The baby, very much alive, was brought to an orphanage run by the nuns of our Order. His grandmother left instructions that he was to be named Richard, but not to be adopted.

The marriage took place and Alice moved to her husband's palatial home. They were happy and Alice had every luxury money could buy. However, after four years of hoping and trying, it became evident that they could not have children. This was a bitter disappointment to both of them. One evening the husband, John, introduced the subject of adoption. Alice agreed but expressed the hope that they could get a baby rather than an older child. They planned to go together to the convent orphanage the following Saturday. At the last minute John was called away on urgent business, so Alice went alone.

By a strange quirk of fate, the headmistress was out that day and a young Sister who did not know the background of the orphans was in temporary charge. Regretfully, she informed Alice that there were no babies available at that time and asked her to call again in two or three months. Seeing the deep disappointment on Alice's face, the young Sister inquired if she had ever considered an older child. Alice explained that she and her husband wanted to train a little one from the beginning as their own son. The eager nun said she understood this but explained that they had a really gorgeous little boy, whom no one had ever adopted. He was, she said, the favourite with all the staff, but for some unknown reason this bright, handsome child was never even shown to prospective parents. More to humour her than anything else, Alice said she would see him.

The young Sister bustled off, grabbed Richard from his playmates, washed his face, gave him a clean T-shirt and brought him to the parlour. She pushed him into the room and closed the door behind him. Alice turned from her place at the large window to see a small boy, an astonishing replica of herself, standing shyly by the door. His first words were heartbreaking: 'Mummy?' he said. 'Where have you been for so long?'

Alice knew in the instant that he was her own son. In her car, she tore down the road to her mother's house to demand the truth, almost speechless with anger and surprise.

After the initial shock, her mother become very cold and distant. 'Get a grip on yourself, girl,' she said. 'What I did was for your own good. You were on the verge of destroying your whole future and disgracing the family name.'

'I'll never forgive you,' Alice answered furiously, 'and I'm going to adopt him immediately.'

'You most certainly are *not*,' her mother replied. 'Think about it. From what you've said, there is no disguising the likeness between you and your son. Your husband will see it immediately and he will divorce you. Do you plan to come back to us with your illegitimate child? Surely you accept that you owe us our good names in this neighbourhood.'

Tragically, Alice saw her mother's reasoning and bitterly agreed to leave the boy in the orphanage. She provided an excellent education for him, but he was never destined to live with her in her grand house as her son and heir.

6

Ready for the Future

After I'd made my First Vows, I was sent to teacher training college in London in 1951, aged eighteen. I was told to choose English literature as my specialist subject and I found the course stimulating and instructive. To be partially back in the 'world' was more than interesting: it was exciting. Another Sister and myself were resident during the week and came back to our convent at weekends.

We were strictly forbidden to leave the college grounds under any pretext, except as part of the course. I remember the almost palpable expectancy that filled the air when the accession to the throne of Queen Elizabeth II was to be proclaimed in St James's Palace. I dithered fearfully. I wanted desperately to attend, but dare I? It was not an educational outing, no matter how I scrutinised it. In the end, I decided that such a historic event was not to be missed.

The proclamation was not far from the college. I could see the crowds gathering and, feeling slightly guilty, I slipped in among them. An impressive little herald in full regalia arose before me and, in stentorian tones, proclaimed: 'The high and mighty Princess Elizabeth Alexandra Mary ... is now become our only lawful and rightful Sovereign.'

The huge and spontaneous applause was heartening. I crept away quietly, exulting that I had been a part of it. I never mentioned my enterprising effort to the powers-that-be! That was the only time I failed in what was called 'Holy Obedience'. The imperative to seek self-denial aided our observance of regulations. We were free, but we had chosen to follow them.

In 1954, I took Final Vows and in the following years remained immersed in the work of the Order. Nevertheless, as time and my twenties went by, I became restless and torn. There was so much in the Order that I loved: the wit, the sheer idealism, the moral stature and the camaraderie of friends around me, the immense compassion for the weak and suffering of our world. I suppose I wasn't brave enough, or spiritual enough. At any rate, I decided in 1964 at the age of thirty-two, that convent life was not for me. Leaving was easy – a new and gentle Irish Reverend Mother suggested I spend a year of 'Exclaustration' back in the world before I made a final decision. I sent my married sister Mary such peculiar measurements for cloth to make dresses that her husband remarked I must be the original A-line.

I found life away from the convent a mixture of drabness and extraordinary novelty. Television was a surprise – and cooking a complete mystery. I went to various parties and dances and to my amazement, after a very short spell of exuding a disingenuous friendliness and perhaps unconscious signals of availability, I received no fewer than five proposals of marriage. This was all the more extraordinary because until I was formally released from my vows I could neither hug nor kiss any of those hopefuls. I think they concluded I was a seriously inhibited but virtuous girl.

At the year's end, I made a final decision and went home to my deeply worried parents. I was a qualified teacher and I could earn my living, but only in the UK. One of my swains was a charming Irishman, but to teach in Ireland, I had to be fluent in the Irish language – so I left him. Once I had parted from the convent, with its major commitments, I found it very easy to leave lesser attractions.

I took up a new teaching career in London and was lucky enough to find my future husband there. Consciously, I put a brake on my drifting and on the exhilaration of being free to choose. I married my English husband and, as in the proverbial fairy tale, have been happy ever after – and thereby hangs another tale!

The family shortly after arrival in
Brookedale in 1937.

Dad – entertaining Mam in the kitchen.

Tea in the hayfield.

The river 'down the glen' where we played.

Dad sharpening a saw. A Jack of all trades.

Any excuse for 'a bit of a ceilidh' in the kitchen . . .

The house my father built.

The shining wonder.